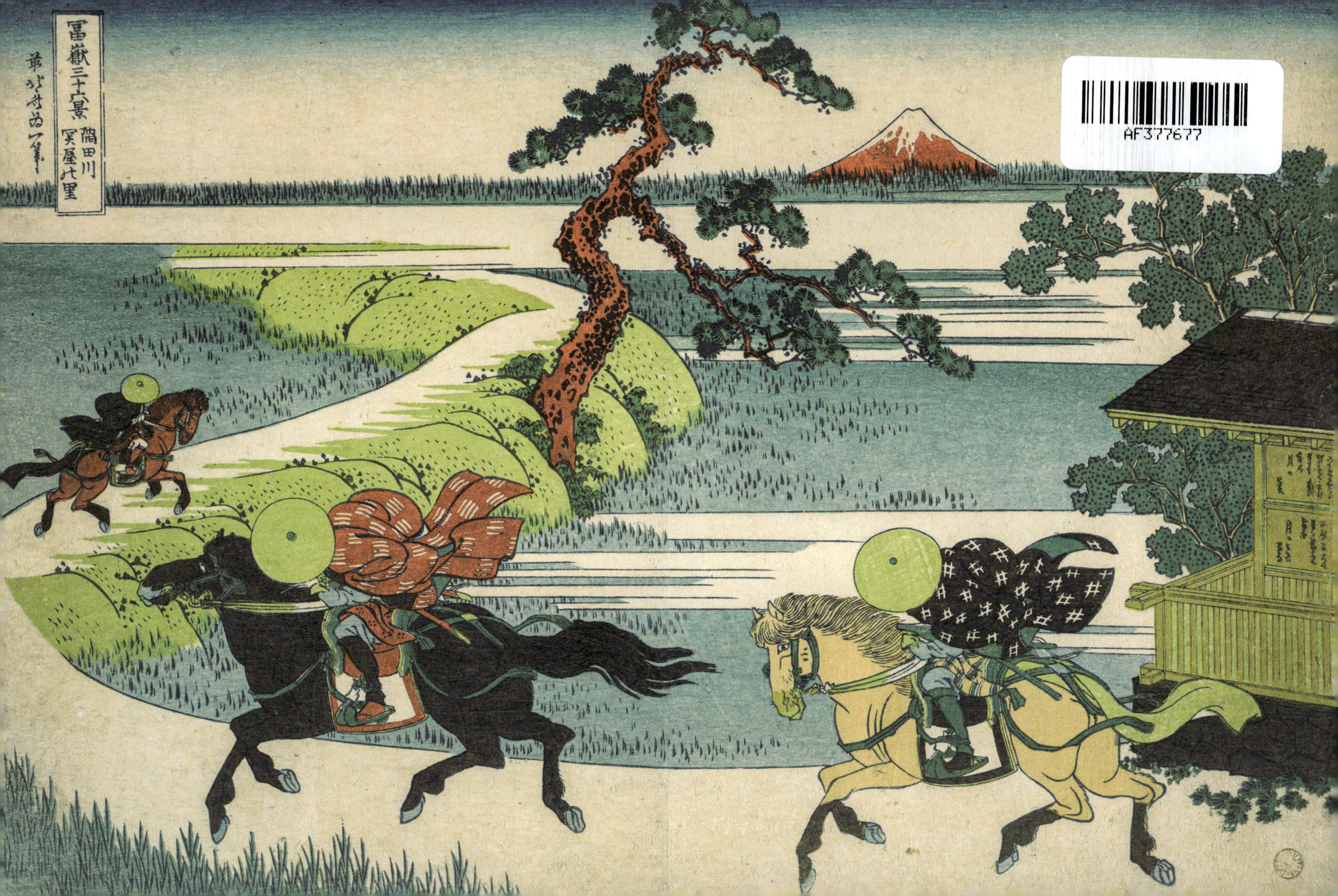
冨嶽三十六景
隅田川關屋の里
前北斎為一筆
AF377677

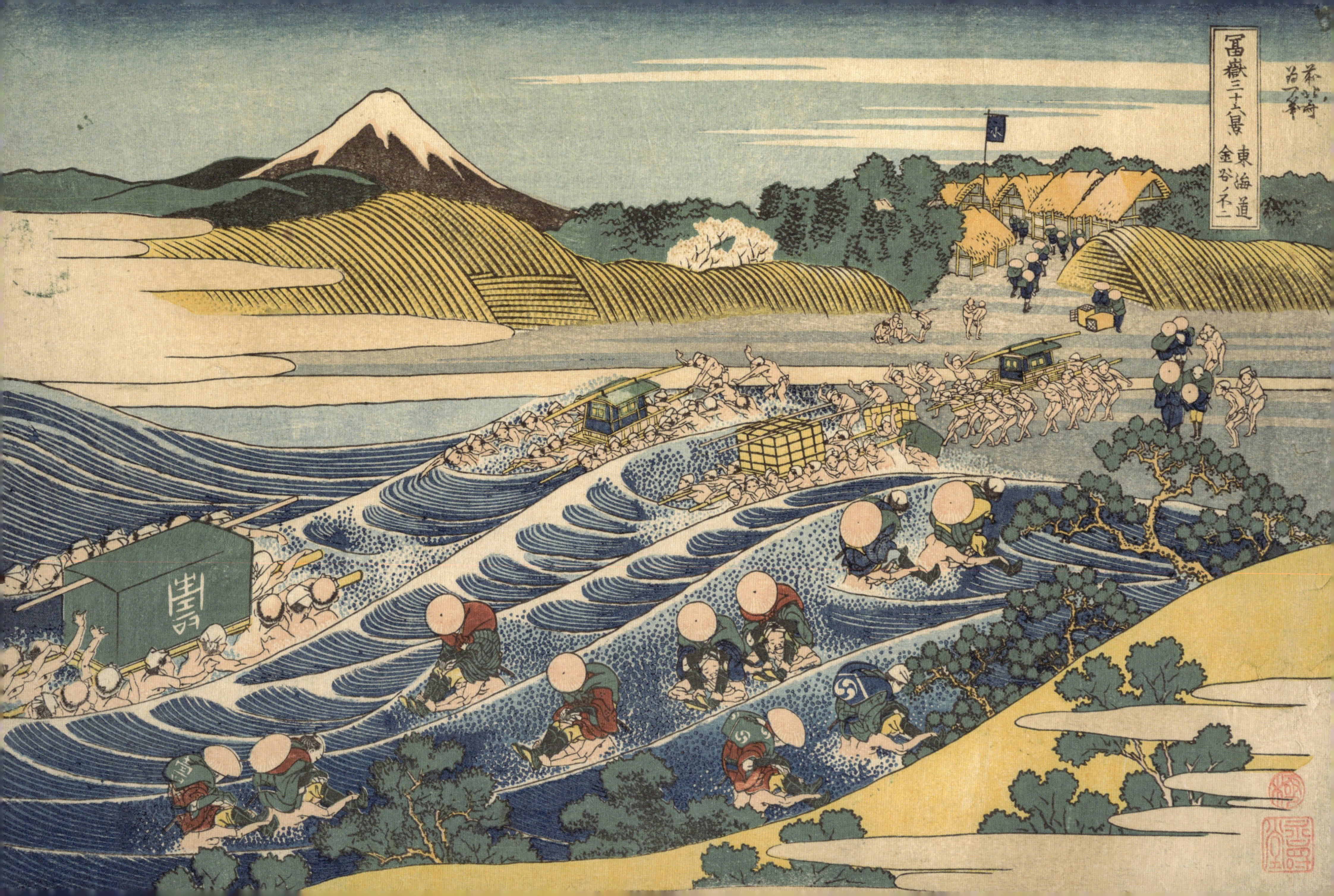

冨嶽三十六景　東海道　金谷ノ不二
前北斎為一筆

Hokusai

THIRTY-SIX VIEWS OF MOUNT FUJI

From the Collection of The Metropolitan Museum of Art, New York

Elisabetta Scantamburlo

TUTTLE Publishing

Tokyo | Rutland, Vermont | Singapore

CONTENTS

PAGE 1
Katsushika Hokusai, *Sekiya Village on the Sumida River (Sumidagawa Sekiya no sato)*, print, ink and color on paper, 10 × 14¼ in (25.4 × 38.7 cm), page 88, #31.

PAGE 2
Katsushika Hokusai, *Fuji Seen From Kanaya on the Tokaido (Tokaido Kanagawa no Fuji)*, print, ink and color on paper, 10¼ ×15¼ in (26 × 38.7 cm), page 118, #45.

PAGES 6–7
Katsushika Hokusai, *South Wind, Clear Sky (Gaifu kaisei)*, print, ink and color on paper (detail), 9⅝ × 14 in (24.4 × 35.6 cm), page 42, #11.

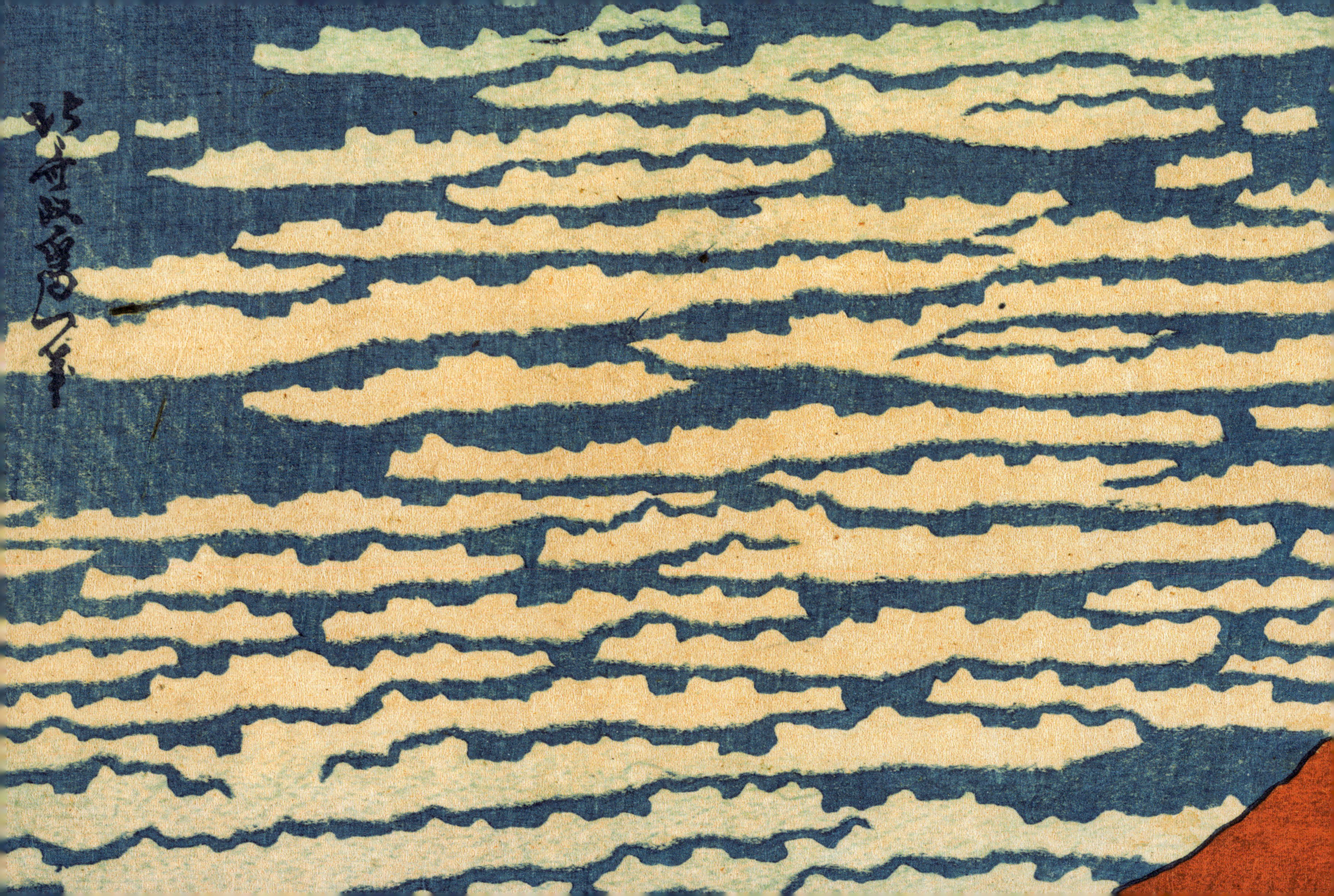
北斎改爲一筆

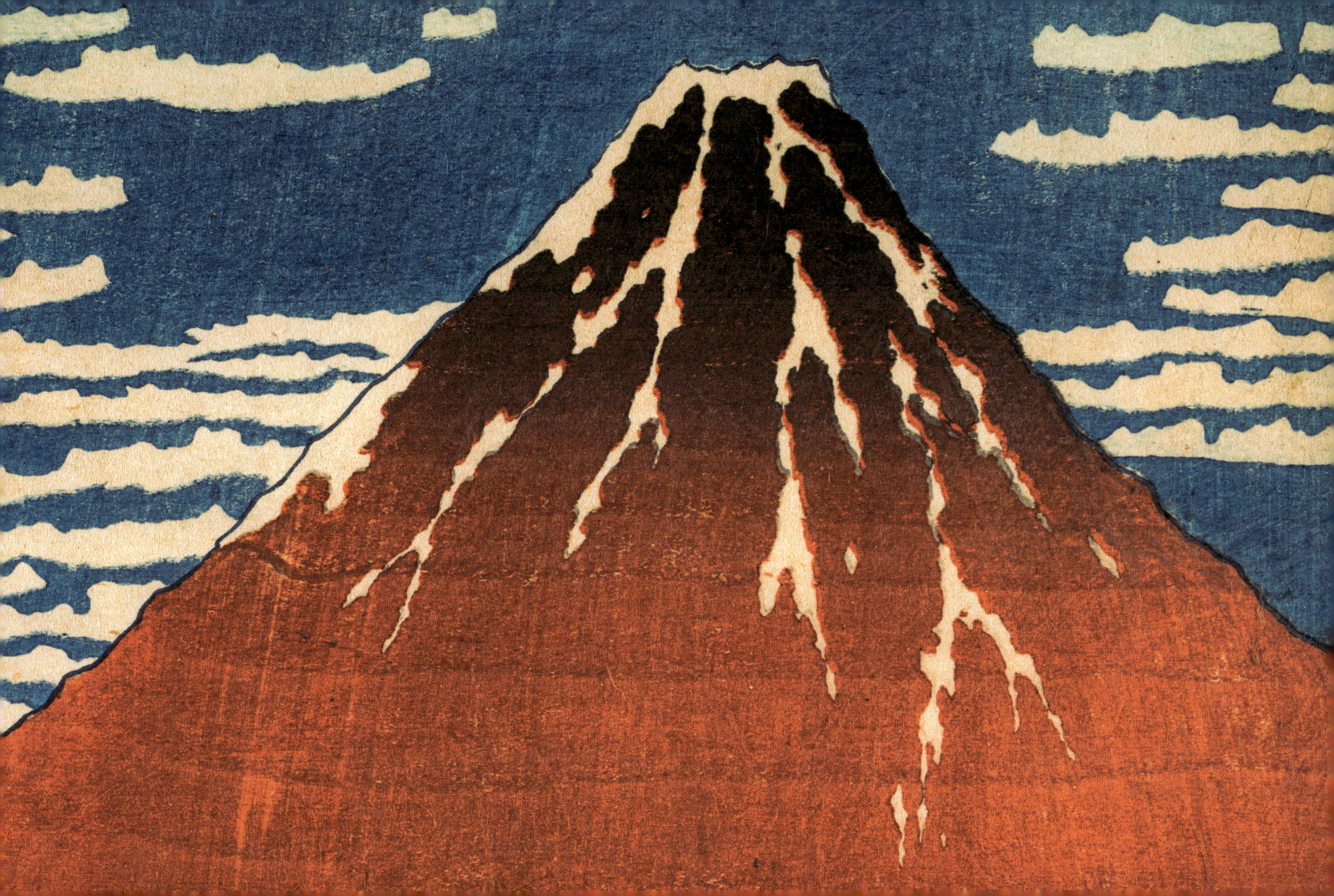

Hokusai's Extraordinary Mt. Fuji Series

The Great Wave by Katsushika Hokusai (#16) is probably the best-known Japanese artwork in the world. Often thought of as a standalone piece, many people do not know that it belongs to a series of forty-six prints dedicated to Mount Fuji—a series that revolutionized the history of Japanese art.

Around 1830, when Hokusai started work on *The Great Wave*, he had already created thousands of works of art. He was trained in the tradition of *ukiyo-e* "floating world images," an artistic movement of the Edo period (1603–1868) and an expression of the new bourgeois urban culture, whose favorite subjects were courtesans, actors and the worlds of pleasure and leisure. The preferred medium was woodblock printing, a technique that was increasingly perfected in this period. Hokusai was seventy years old when he began the series *Thirty-six Views of Mount Fuji* (*Fugaku sanjurokkei*). The prints bear no dates; these have to be inferred from various elements, such as the signatures. All the works are signed by Hokusai with the pen name Iitsu, which he had assumed in 1820 but later changed to Manji in 1834. It is therefore assumed that he delivered the drawings to the publisher before 1834. However, this does not preclude the possibility that they may have been printed after 1834.

Although Hokusai was already an established artist, he never stopped seeking to improve his skills and constantly sought out new challenges. He changed his name several times throughout his long career, as if wanting to be reborn each time as a new artist with greater experience and a renewed curiosity. There was no area of nature or the human experience that he had not explored through paintings, prints, illustrated books, cards, pamphlets and large-scale works. As a *ukiyo-e* artist, he depicted actors, female beauty, landscapes, ordinary people and even erotic images (*shunga*). He also made an important, original contribution to the genre of manga—educational sketchbook manuals for beginners and professional artists which investigated nature, humanity and the supernatural. In 1814, at age the age of 55 (the Japanese count one year of age at birth), Hokusai began the unprecedented feat of drawing thousands of images for 15 volumes of manga; the last two were published posthumously in 1878. It is thus no surprise that a man with such indomitable character and spirit would at the ripe old age of 70 create his most iconic and memorable series.

What makes *Thirty-six Views of Mount Fuji* so extraordinary is not only the artist's ability and vision, but also the fact that at the time landscapes were not yet considered as a principal subject for woodblock prints. Previously, landscapes had been represented in paintings in the classical style. These were often born from the imagination of the artist and from interpretations of iconic forms rather than as representations of actual places. In prints of the earlier Edo period, they appear as backgrounds to the main subjects—actors, beautiful women, courtesans and scenes from the theater or pleasure quarters. The landscape only becomes a subject in its own right in the first half of the 19th century. This was fueled by the search for new themes to entice the sales of prints resulting from increased competition between publishers, and the fact that traditional subjects were increasingly liable to censorship claims, particularly erotic images or portraits of recognizable courtesans and actors. Just as the *ukiyo-e* was losing its vitality, Hokusai's series breathed new life into the genre.

Another element that contributed to the success of the series was the increase in domestic travel within Japan, which spurred an interest in the destinations one could visit. Images of those places became souvenirs that allowed one to envision their actual or potential trips. After declaring *sakoku* in 1642 (the total closure of Japan to the outside world), the shogunate had restricted domestic travel within Japan. However, by the early 19th century the government was in decline and the population was unhappy with its restrictions, especially with the censorship it had enforced for nearly two centuries. Following the easing of these prohibitions, people were finally able to move and travel around the country freely.

In fact, it was during this period that the government built the five great roads (Gokaido) that connected Edo (today's Tokyo) to Kyoto through the west and to Nikko through the northeast; their stations would become new subjects for artists. Traversed by merchants, pilgrims and leisure travelers, these routes also made travel safer. The beginning of the 19th century thus witnessed a rapid increase in domestic travel which facilitated new connections between city dwellers and nature as well as a rediscovery of Shinto and Buddhist sites.

Hokusai and his publisher Nishimuraya Yohachi, whose publishing house Eijudo was among the most influential of the time, conceived a major new project: the first ever print series dedicated entirely to natural beauty. When Hokusai took on this project, he carried with him a wealth of experience, a refined style and an artistic eye and

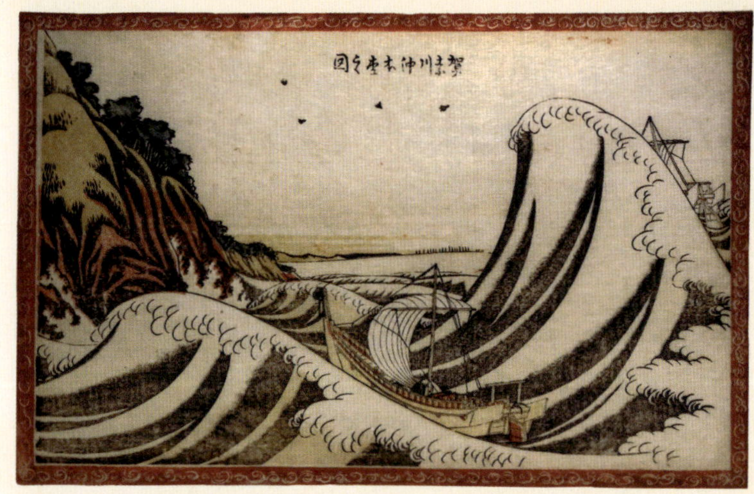

spirit. Leveraging these assets, he was able to seamlessly connect each landscape image to the emotions that he wished to convey with a sense of spontaneity and directness.

His novel conception of landscapes as an independent artistic subject completely transformed its role in the history of *ukiyo-e*. Naturally, this was not the first time Hokusai had devoted himself to the subject. He had already created *sansuiga* paintings ("pictures of mountains and water") in the Chinese style. At the beginning of the nineteenth century, he had also attempted to depict some landscapes in a Western style borrowing Dutch techniques (see pages 10–11). His mastery of these techniques however came to fruition in *Thirty-six Views of Mount Fuji* where his images appeared completely new to Japanese audiences yet recognizable to those in the West. The relative novelty of the subject matter and the originality of the depictions, as well as his mastery of execution, brought immediate success to the genre and the series, which would later see the addition of ten prints for a total of forty-six.

In 1830, in a volume book published by Nishimuraya titled the

Stories in a Promptbook Form (Shohon jitate), an advertisement appeared announcing the release of the *Thirty-six Views of Mount Fuji*: "...work of old man Iitsu, formerly Hokusai, in single *aizuri-e* sheets, one view per sheet. These images show how the shape of Fuji changes according to the perspective from which it is viewed (...). The blocks will be carved one after the other, and may reach a hundred." The same advertisement appears in six other volumes published by Nishimuraya in 1831. It seems that the last prints of the original series were released in 1832 and the additional ten in 1833. The first thirty-six prints in this volume follow the order identified by art historian Andreas Marks, who relied heavily on censor and publisher seals, advertisements from printed books, and Hokusai's various signatures.

It is impossible to know exactly how many copies were printed by Nishimuraya. There were certainly many; for example, it is estimated that *The Great Wave* was printed between 5000 and 8000 times, though not all images were as popular. In some cases, the print blocks had to be modified or replaced with new ones, so a variety of distinct versions can be found with different colors and variations in details.

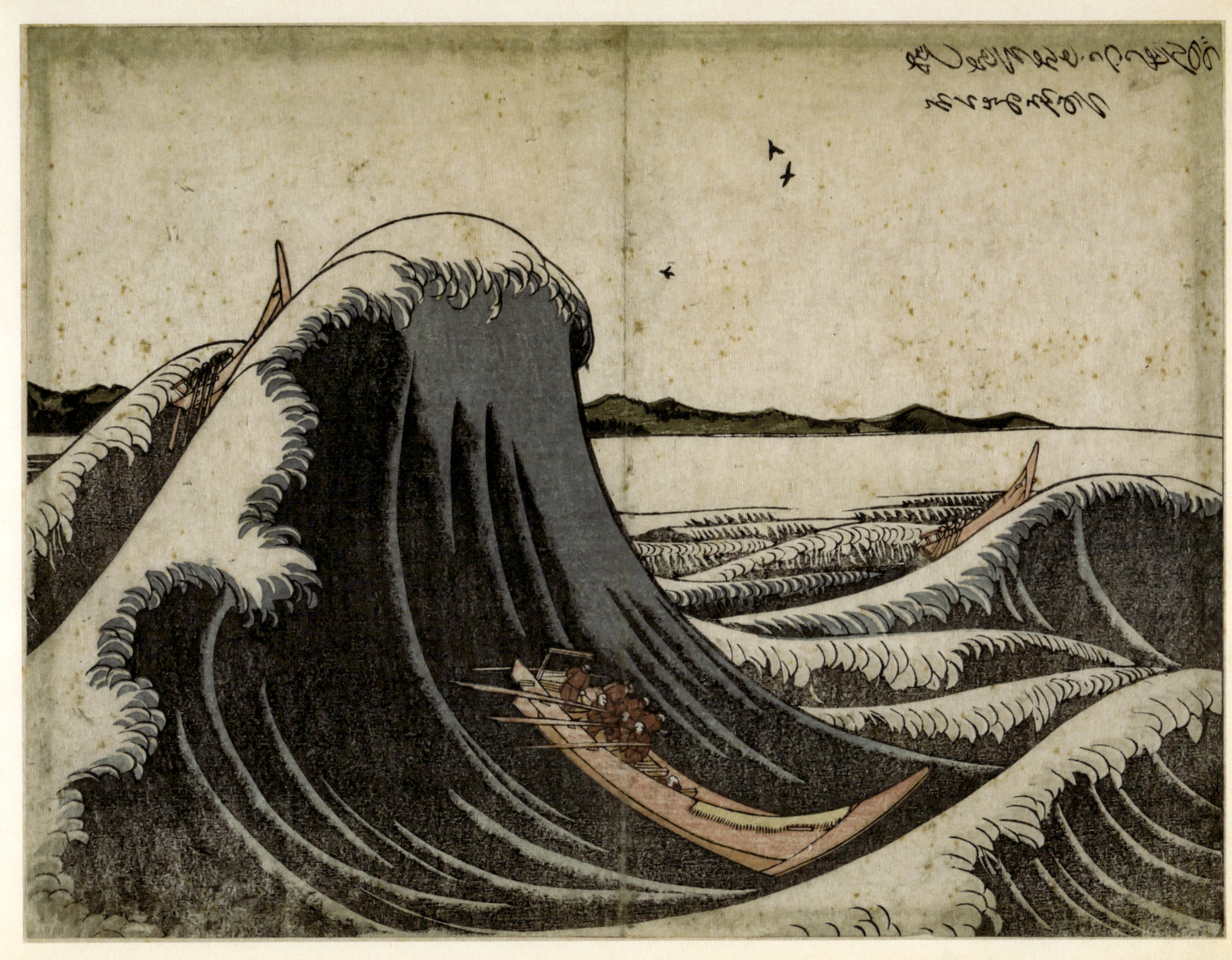

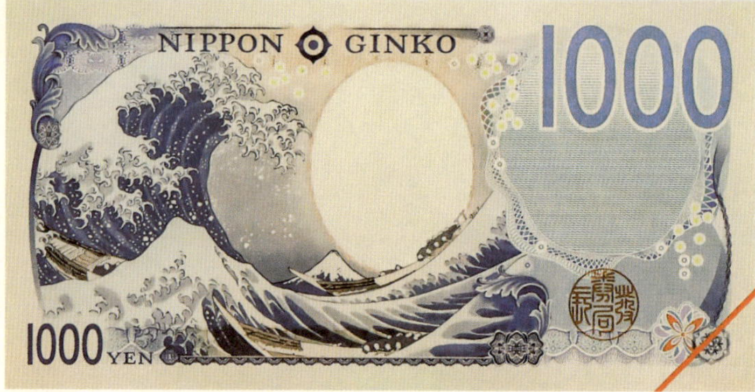

Sacred Mount Fuji

Mt. Fuji is an active volcano 12,389 feet (3776 meters) high with a crater 2,560 feet (780 meters) across. Located 62 miles (100 kilometers) southwest of Tokyo, it has a symmetrical conical shape and its summit is covered in snow for five months of the year. Created by successive lava flows starting more than 100,000 years ago, it is one of three sacred mountains in Japan (along with Mount Haku and Mount Tate). Considered sacred in *shinto* Japanese beliefs, entrance to Fuji was forbidden to women like many other sacred places in Japan; the ban was lifted in 1872, allowing women to climb the mountain for religious or leisurely purposes. Ironically, it was a woman by the name of Princess Konohanasakuya who served as the goddess of this mountain and of all volcanoes in Japan, according to the *Nihon Shoki* ("Chronicles of Japan," written in 720).

In 2013, Fuji was designated a UNESCO World Heritage Site. Celebrated in literature, poetry and art, Fuji continues to inspire Japanese artists today, including many contemporary painters and designers. Hokusai's Fuji now even appears on the new 1,000-yen banknote. According to the tradition of *hatsuyume* ("first dream"), dreaming of Fuji on the first night of the year is a sign of good fortune in the year to come.

During the period when the Hokusai print series was created, the sacred mountain attracted many pilgrims. In the earlier Edo period, Fuji was also the object of worship by religious groups called *Fujiko*, whose activities included ascents up the sacred mountain. Miniature models (*Fujizuka*) of the mountain were even built around the city of Edo for those who could not travel there. Today, the volcano is climbed for both religious and recreational purposes and as soon as the mountain opens on June 1st of every year, many groups race to make it to the summit.

In Japanese, the mountain is called *Fujisan* not *Fujiyama* (富士山); *san* and *yama* are two readings of the character 山 for "mountain." The characters that today and for centuries have been used to write Fuji are 富 ("wealth, fortune") and 士 ("man of rank"), but the original meaning of the name remains lost. A possible origin could be found in *The Tale of the Bamboo Cutter (Taketori Monogatari)*, a 10th-century tale in which an elixir of life, burned on the mountaintop, is given the name *fushi* (不死, "immortal"). A variant then sees the use of the characters 不二 ("unique, unparalleled"), used also in some of the prints in this series.

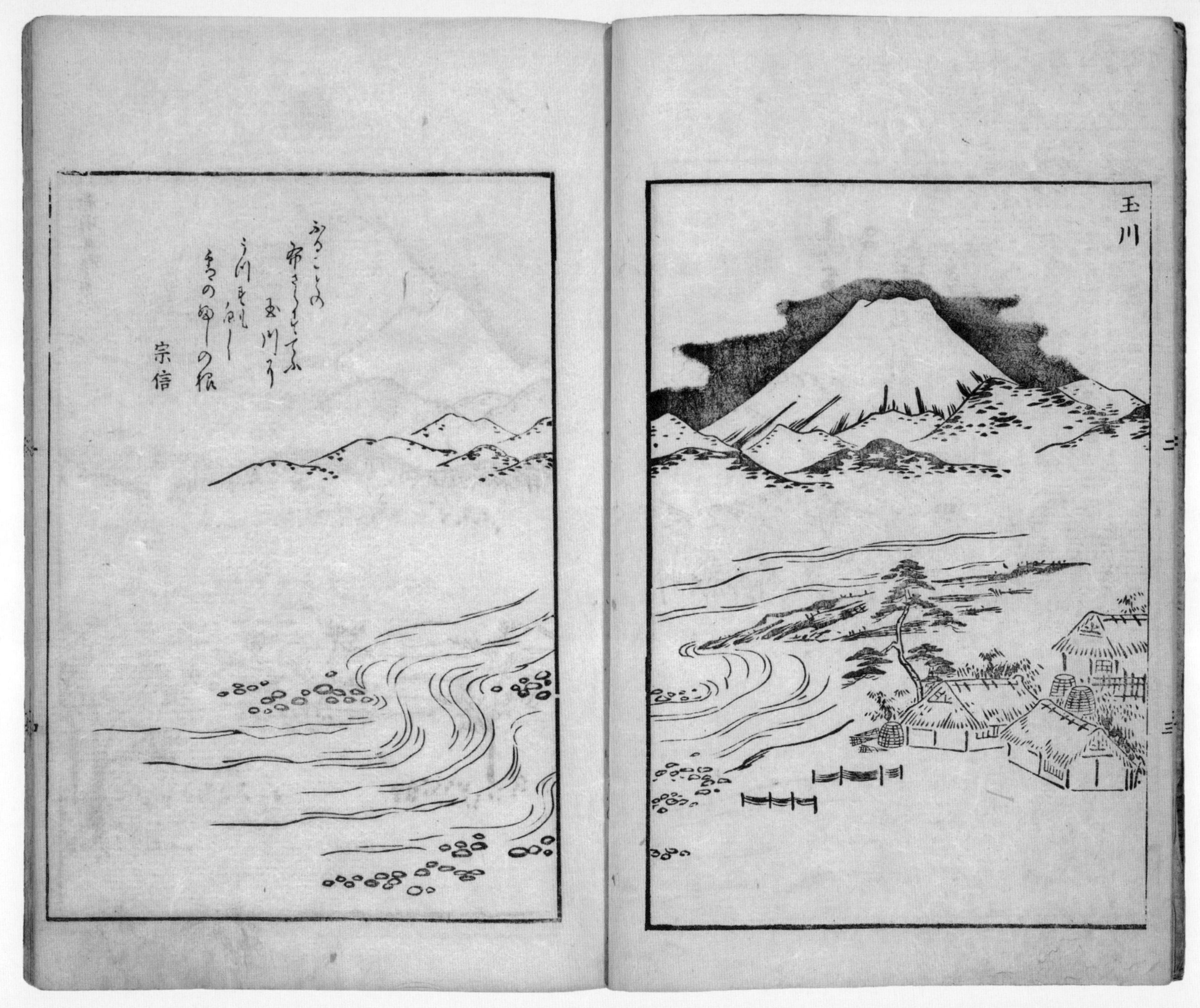
玉川
宗信

Representing Mount Fuji with New Techniques

It seems that the more "the old fool" tried to represent reality, the more it escaped him. In a kind of incessant eagerness to penetrate the world around him, Hokusai became obsessed with the great sacred mountain, whose seemingly simple symmetry was precisely the source of its enigmatic complexity. His desire to know the mountain from every point of view, at every moment or day of the year, was the need to arrive at a meaning—an essence perhaps at the heart of art and life itself. Hokusai was indeed known to be eccentric in character, ever at the edge of insanity. Although his originality is undeniable, it must be said that one of his inspirations for the series was Kawamura Minsetsu's *Hundred Views of Mount Fuji (Hyaku Fuji).* Active around the mid-18th century, Minsetsu first published his work in four volumes in 1767 from a series of sketches he made of the volcano during his travels.

Hokusai borrowed elements from Minsetsu and other sources, following the common practice of drawing inspiration from (and even copying) earlier works of art, which was accepted in the Edo period. Hokusai thus depicts Fuji from a myriad of different aspects—different seasons, times of day and places of observation, at various distances and with many local customs and habits. Although the titles of the individual prints give an indication of the places from which one could enjoy the views shown, these are not always accurate, for the artist often fused imagination and memory with reality to achieve a desired effect. Many of the images are set at post stations along one of the five main routes that ran across Japan (the Gokaido): the Tokaido, Nakasendo, Koshu Kaido, Oshu Kaido and Nikko Kaido. The artist masterfully uses geometric shapes, Western perspective and traditional Japanese representation, symmetry, shadows and light, static lines and movement.

From a technical point of view, the defining feature of the series and one of the main reasons for its success was its prevalent use of Prussian blue. Created in Germany in 1704 and imported to Japan in 1829, it was the first synthetic pigment in history. Owing to its intense color, Prussian blue was immediately preferred to natural blue dyes extracted from the *Commelina* flower or *Indigofera tinctoria* (from which indigo is obtained), which were both used in *ukiyo-e* at the time.

The public was enamored by this novel shade of blue that they had never before seen, which also proved to be more stable and less prone to fading. In the original version of the series, the first five prints were pure *aizuri-e* (with blue tones only), of which only a few examples remain. The second five were partly-*aizuri-e* with light tones of other colors added, like yellow and red. Later versions included more colors. The first thirty-six originals used blue outlines, while the additional ten prints had black outlines. Despite its initial success, *aizuri-e* went out of fashion as other pigments became more readily available. For this reason, subsequent reprints of the *Thirty-six Views of Mount Fuji* were all made in the *nishiki-e* format, which included more colors.

Another element that contributed to the success of the series was the frequent use of *bokashi* shading, a technique adopted by the engraver that allowed for the creation of gradations and deeper hues. Instead of being applied uniformly, color was blended onto a wet wooden mold. The process had to be repeated for each print.

Hokusai's compositions of the individual images were organized according to simple geometric principles: shapes that were similar to Fuji were repeated at different points in the print using basic elements that changed each time. In some cases, Fuji is the undisputed protagonist of the print. In others, it is as if the artist wants to challenge us by hiding the mountain among buildings, nature or human activity. Whether covered or not in snow, its silent presence remains unchanged through time and seasons, a witness to the passing of earthly joys and concerns. The mountain remains a constant participant in a larger story; scenes unfold in front of it that touch on the humorous and laborious, alternating between forces of nature that threaten to disrupt and tranquil scenes that soothe the spirit. Above all, Fuji reigns in silence. Despite their separate and distinct characteristics, nature and humanity converge around a shared essence that is at once earthly and divine. In the *Thirty-six Views of Mount Fuji*, Hokusai captures that liminal space between the eternal and the transitory, the sacred and the profane, fusing them until there is no longer any boundary or separation.

The *Thirty-six Views of Mount Fuji* series is an artist's love song to one of Japan's most iconic symbols, past and present, invoking a kaleidoscope of literary, artistic and religious references while creating new ones. With this series, Hokusai changed perceptions of Fuji and turned it into an even more beloved symbol of Japanese life.

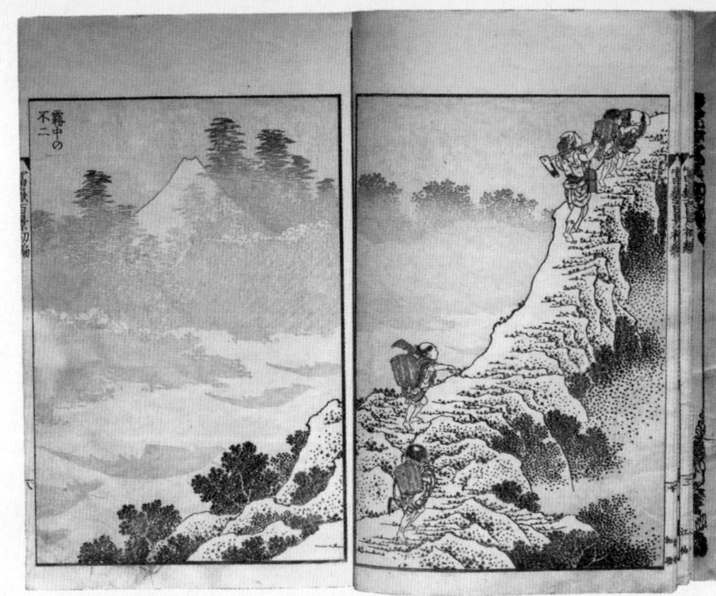

Katsushika Hokusai, *Fuji in Mist (Muchu no Fuji)*, from the series *One Hundred Views of Mount Fuji (Fugaku hyakkei)*, vol. I #9, print, ink on paper, 8¹⁵⁄₁₆ × 6¼ in (22.7 × 15.8 cm), 1834–1835.

The Great Success of the Series

The success of the series was immediate, as was the decision to add ten more prints for a total of forty-six. But it was not enough. In the following years, Hokusai was to devote himself again to Fuji with the series *One Hundred Views of Mount Fuji (Fugaku hyakkei)*—though it was actually 102—spread across three volumes published in 1834–1835 (Volumes I and II) and in the 1840s (Volume III).

Hokusai's work also inspired other great artists such as Hiroshige, who between 1833 and 1834 produced a landscape series entitled *The Fifty-Three Stations of the Tokaido Road (Tokaido gojusan tsugi)* to immediate success. It is possible that Nishimuraya's decision to add ten additional prints was in response to the competition between the two great artists. Hokusai and Nishimuraya did not get around to making 100 views immediately as they had announced, but devoted themselves to other landscape and travel series to vary the offerings.

These included: *A Tour of Waterfalls in Various Provinces (Shokoku taki meguri*, 1833–1834); *Remarkable Views of Bridges in Various Provinces (Shokoku meikyo kiran*, c. 1834); *A True Mirror of Chinese and Japanese Poetry (Shika shashin kyo*, 1833–1834) and *One Hundred Poems Explained by a Nurse (Hyakunin isshu uba ga etoki*, 1835–1836).

Although less popular than the original series, critics consider *One Hundred Views* the magnum opus of Hokusai's landscapes. While the *Thirty-six Views* include large single sheets printed in color, the *One Hundred Views* were smaller works printed in black and gray, and brought together in three volumes. Having already achieved masterpiece status with the first series, the new series was later popularized with the release of inexpensive versions of a lower quality. In the afterword to the *One Hundred Views of Mount Fuji*, Hokusai wrote:

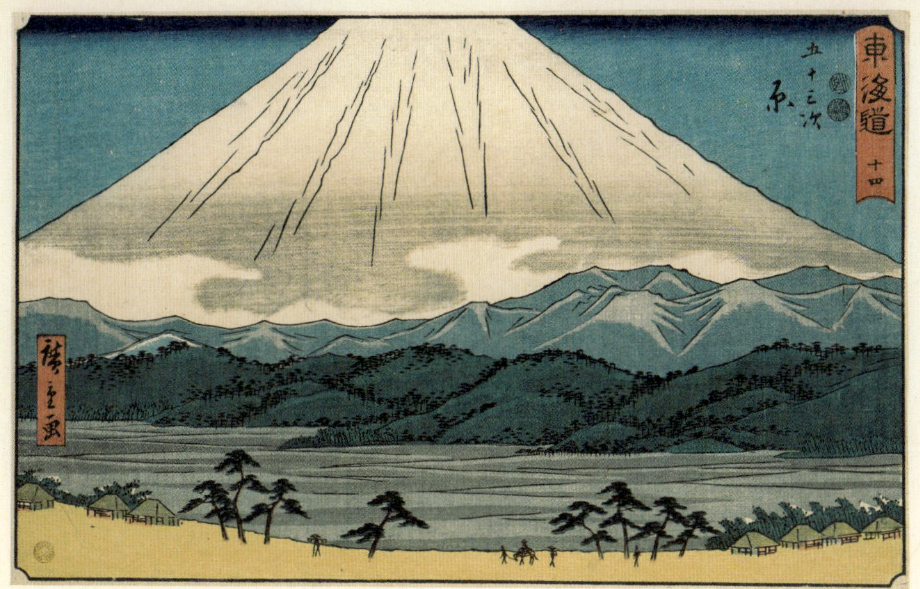

LEFT
Utagawa Hiroshige, *Hara #14*, from the series *The Fifty-Three Stations of the Tokaido Road (Tokaido gojusan tsugi)*, print, ink and color on paper, 8¾ × 13¾ in (22.2 × 34.9 cm), 1833–1834.

BOTTOM
Utagawa Hiroshige, *Numazu #13*, from the series *The Fifty-Three Stations of the Tokaido Road (Tokaido gojusan tsugi)*, print, ink, and color on paper, 10 × 14¾ in (25.1 × 37.5 cm), 1833–1834.

From the age of 6, I had a mania for drawing the shapes of things. When I was 50, I had published a universe of designs. But all I have done before the age of 70 is not worth bothering with. At 75, I'll have learned something of the pattern of nature, of animals, of plants, of trees, birds, fish and insects. When I am 80, you will see real progress. At 90, I will have cut my way deeply into the mystery of life itself. At 100, I shall be a marvelous artist. At 110, everything I create—a dot, a line—will jump to life as never before. To all of you who are going to live as long as I do, I promise to keep my word. I am writing this in my old age. I used to call myself Hokusai, but today, I sign myself as Manji, "The Old Man Mad About Drawing."

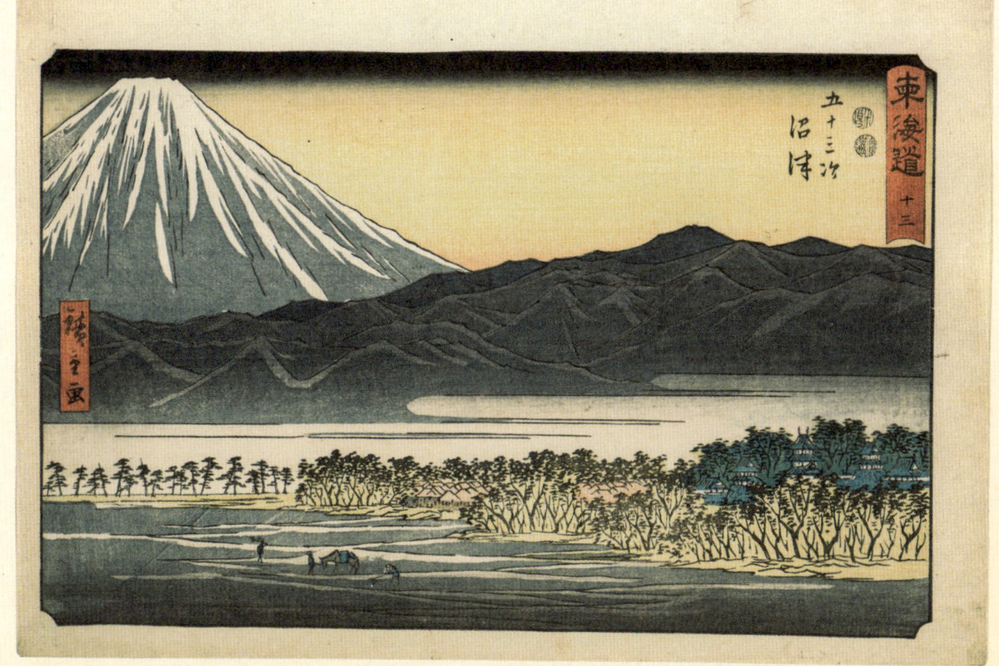

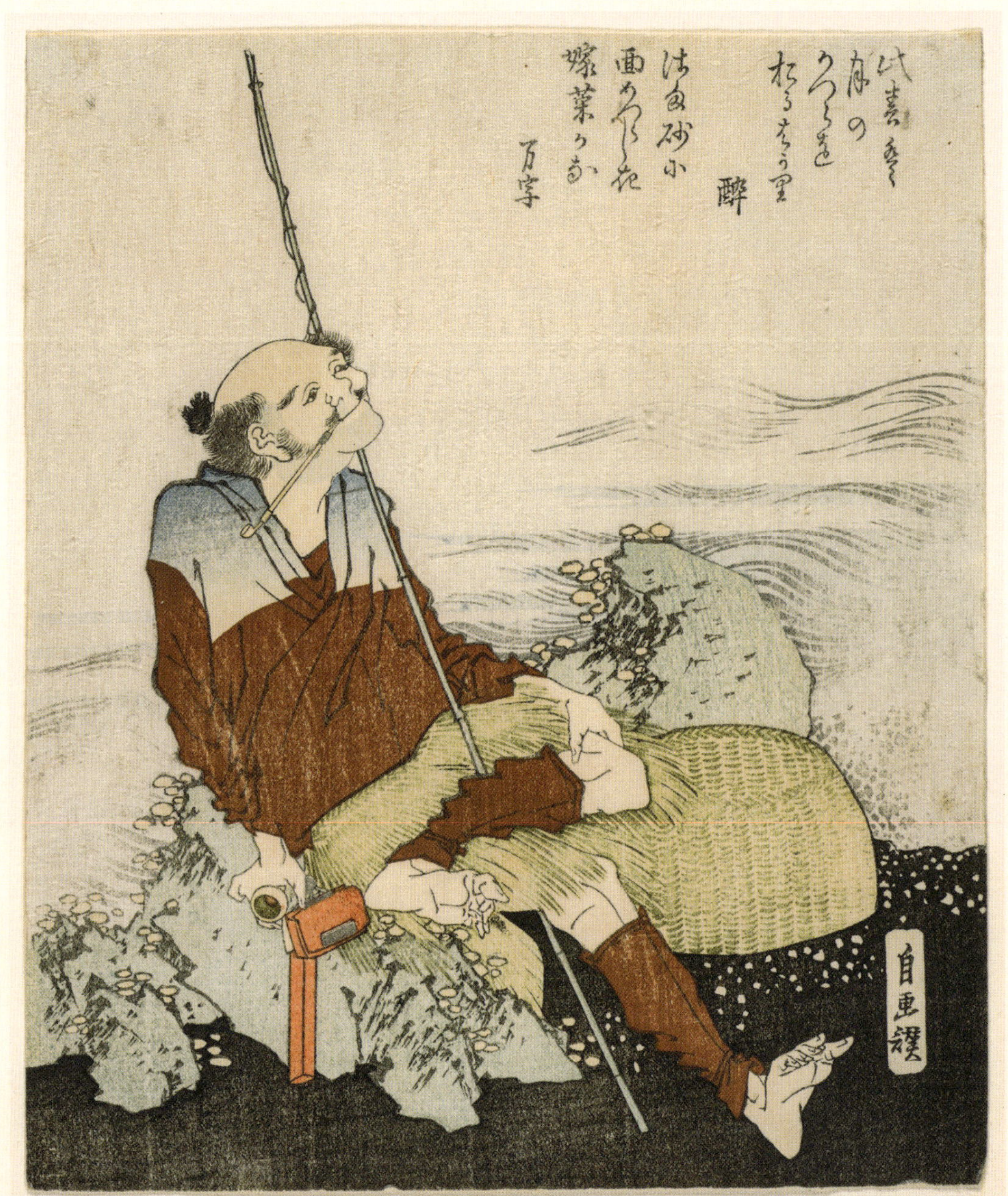

Katsushika Hokusai, *Self-Portrait as a Fisherman*, print, ink, color and metallic pigments on paper, 8⅜ × 7⁵⁄₁₆ in (21.3 × 18.5 cm), 1835.

Notes

PRINT TITLES
The title is given for each print in the series, but the following data common to all works are omitted:
– **date**: c. 1830–1834
– **technique**: polychrome print, ink and color on paper
– **measurements**: *oban* format, approximately 10 × 15 in (25 × 38 cm)
– **credit line**: all prints in the series published in this volume belong to the collection of The Metropolitan Museum of Art in New York with the exception of #30, which is from the collection of the Minneapolis Institute of Art (Mia).

ORDER OF THE PRINTS
The original sequence of the prints in the series and exact dating of each is uncertain. For the first thirty-six prints in this book, the order used is that of Andreas Marks in his book *Hokusai: Thirty-six Views of Mount Fuji (2021)*.

ERAS OF JAPANESE HISTORY
Nara 710–794
Heian 794–1185
Kamakura 1185–1333
Nanbokucho 1334–1392
Muromachi 1392–1573
Azuchi-Momoyama 1573–1600
Edo 1603–1868

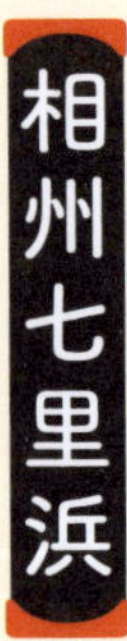

Shichirigahama in Sagami Province

Soshu Shichirigahama

In the foreground we see Shichirigahama ("Shichiri Beach"), and in the center is Enoshima, a small island in Kanagawa Prefecture with large, massive trees. In the distance is snow-covered Mount Fuji with clouds rising on the horizon.

This print, which contains no human elements, is a perfect example of *sansuiga*, a term that describes the landscape painting genre in Japan whose characters signify "mountains" (*san* 山) and "water" (*sui* 水). Only the fishing village of Koshigoe is visible in the middle right.

It is winter and snow covers Fuji and the roofs of the houses. The hill in the lower right mimics the shape of Fuji. In front of the village, the white sea opens up into a vast expanse, rippled by a few small waves. The same white on the right side represents a fog bank. Mount Fuji, on the upper right side, blends into the landscape below. The main colors of the print are shades of blue and green, with pinkish accents in the clouds in the background. The pervasive presence of the Prussian blue tones binds the whole scene together.

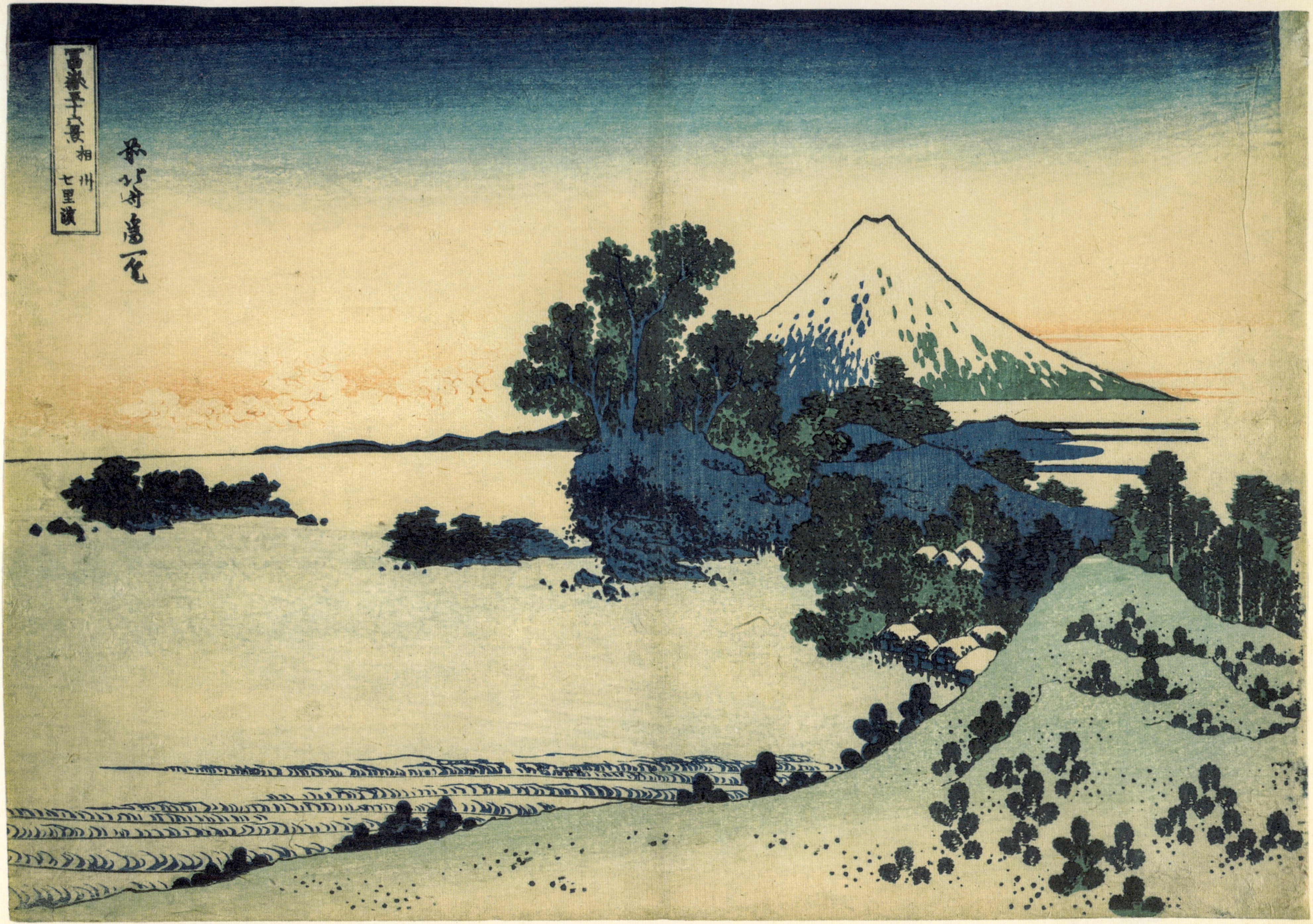

冨嶽三十六景
相州
七里濱

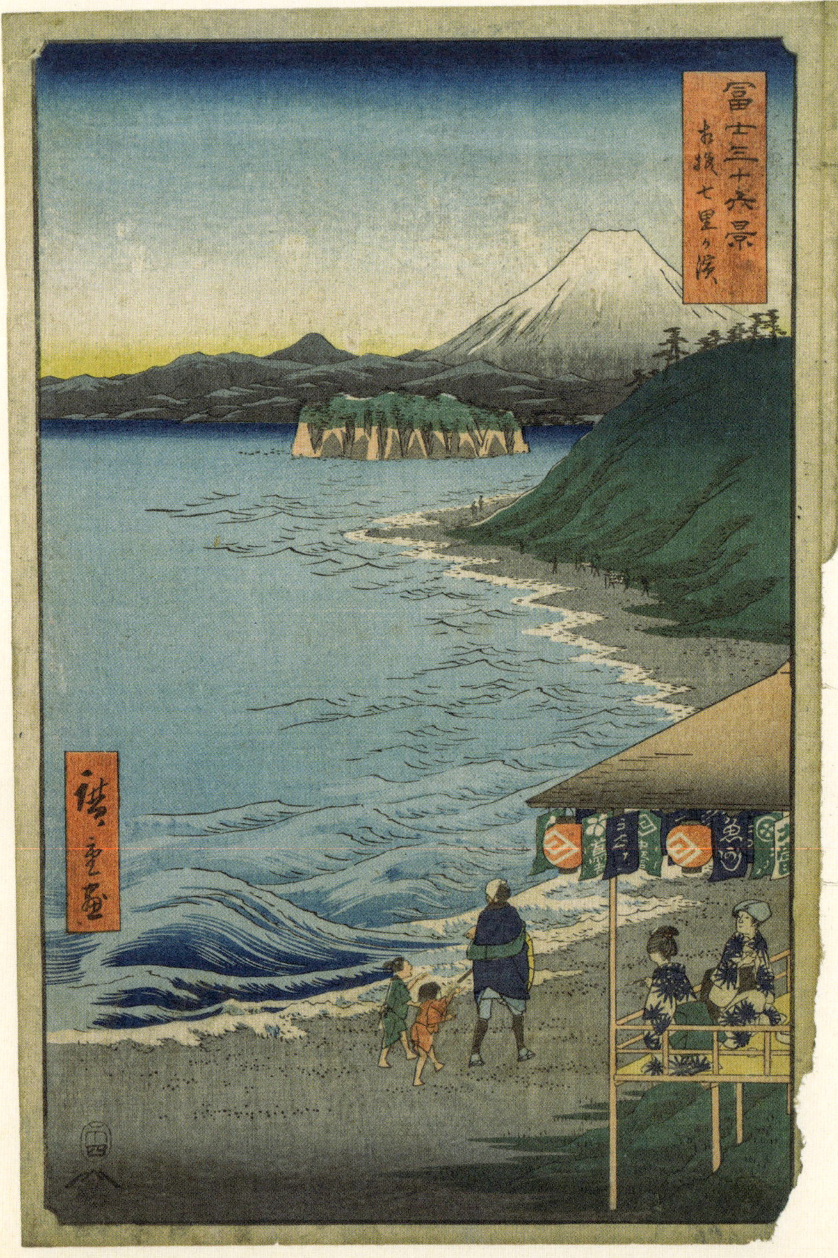

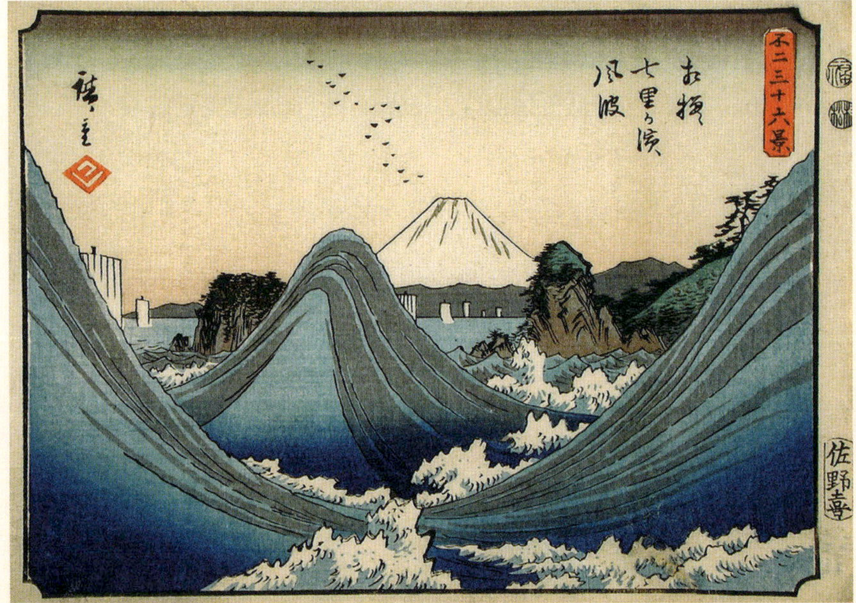

Shichiri Beach is located near Kamakura in Kanagawa Prefecture, southeast of Tokyo. Enoshima Island is a well-known pilgrimage site for devotees of Benzaiten, one of the seven deities of fortune. In the Edo period, the place was a popular subject for *ukiyo-e* artists such as Hiroshige, who also included it in his two *Thirty-six Views of Mount Fuji* (1852 and 1858) series that followed Hokusai's. Even today one can enjoy the view of Fuji from here.

LEFT
Utagawa Hiroshige, *Shichiri Beach in Sagami Province* (*Soshu Shichirigahama*), from the series *Thirty-six Views of Mount Fuji* (*Fugaku sanjurokkei*), print, ink and color on paper, 13⅞ × 9¼ in (35.2 × 23.5 cm), 1858.

ABOVE
Utagawa Hiroshige, *Rough Sea at Shichirigahama in Sagami Province* (*Sagami shichirigahama fuha*), from the series *Thirty-six Views of Mount Fuji* (*Fuji sanjurokkei*), print, ink and color on paper, 7⅛ in × 10 in (18.1 × 25.24 cm), c. 1852.

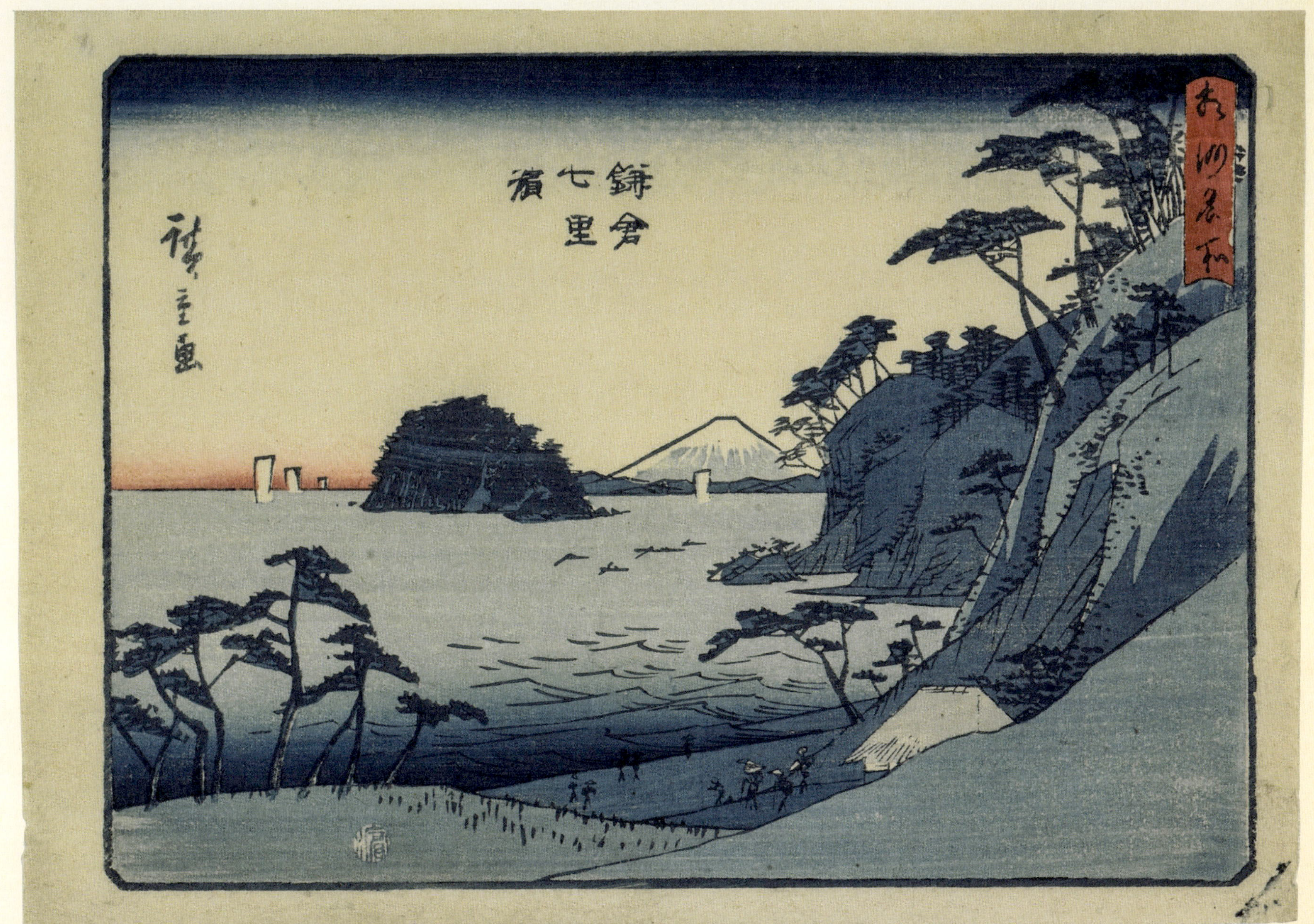

Utagawa Hiroshige, *Shichirigahama Beach in Kamakura* (*Kamakura Shichirigahama*), from the series *Famous Views in Sagami Province* (*Soshu meisho*), print, ink and color on paper, 6¹³⁄₁₆ × 9⁷⁄₁₆ in (17.3 × 23.9 cm), c. 1843–1847.

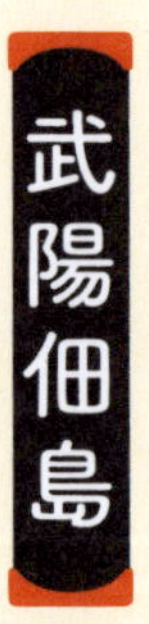

Tsukudajima in Musashi Province

Buyo Tsukudajima

In Hokusai's time, Tsukudajima was a small island on the Sumida River in Tokyo Bay—it remains in existence today. At the end of the 16th century, fisherman from a village called Tsukuda in Settsu Province (present-day Osaka Prefecture) aided *shogun* Tokugawa Ieyasu in his ascent to power. In return, he invited thirty-four fishing families to move to Edo in 1644, granting them this island and naming it after their former village.

The print perfectly captures the busy activity of the fishermen around the island, their various boats loaded with goods of all types. The boat in the foreground, with its bales of cotton, parallels the silhouette and color of the snow-capped Fuji. Hokusai included boats in many prints in the series, often depicting them in detail. This work shows us a wide variety of them, from the small rowboats and ferries in the foreground to the larger ships in the distance. The shapes of the masts and roofs of the island's houses mimic the shape of the volcano, while many of the boats seem to point directly at it.

Hokusai delineates the horizon with a slight curve and observes the island from an elevated perspective. The sky is pink, but the island of Tsukuda is rendered with a deep blue that evokes an evening mood.

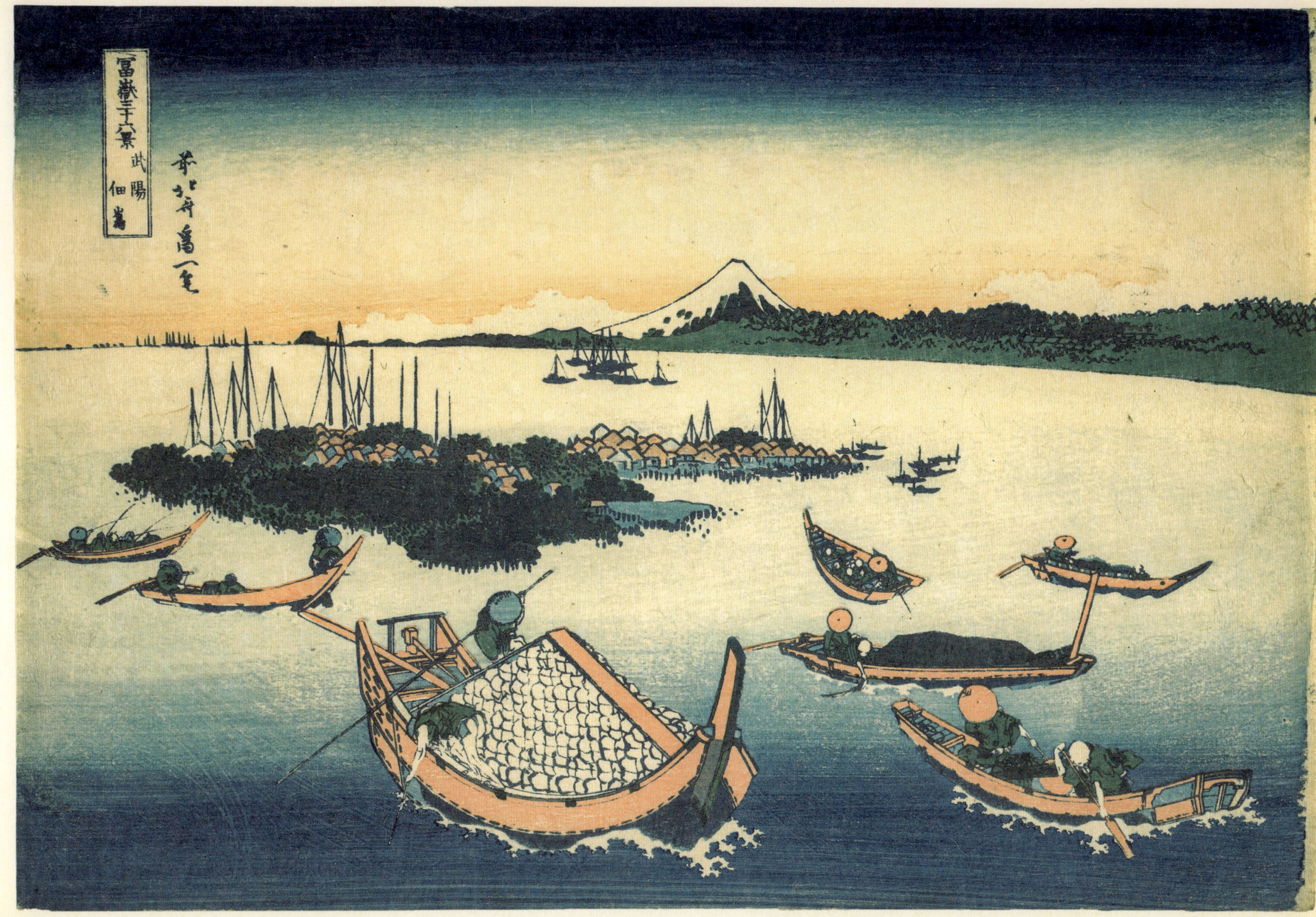

冨嶽三十六景
武陽
佃嶌
北斎為一筆

3

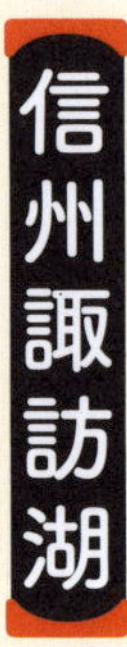

Lake Suwa in Shinano Province

Shinshu Suwako

Fuji appears in the distance behind other mountains. In the foreground a wooden structure, most probably a shrine, is perched on a rock with protruding pine trees that bifurcate the print in two. The roof of the hut resembles the silhouette of Fuji. This technique, often used by Hokusai, establishes a symbolic link between the sacredness of Fuji and that of the shrine. In other cases, the link juxtaposes the eternal spirit of Fuji with the mortal existence of humans.

On the left one catches a glimpse of Takashima Castle in Suwa, present-day Nagano Prefecture in central Honshu, the main island of the Japanese archipelago. The castle today sits further inland; it is likely that the waters of Lake Suwa have receded since Hokusai's time. The area around Lake Suwa was known for its clean air, which the artist depicted through the exclusive use of blue tones and his newly-acquired mastery of Western perspective.

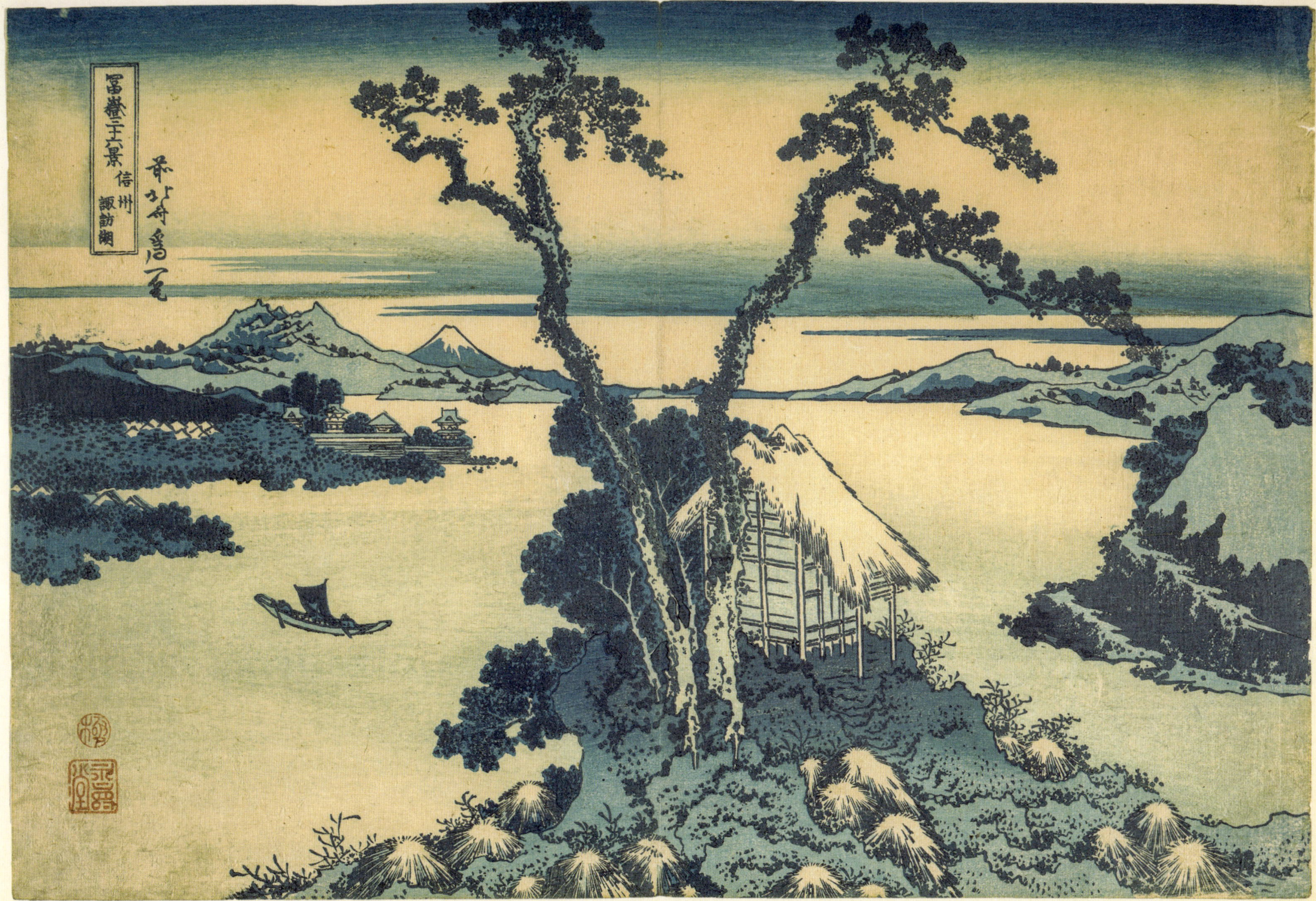

冨嶽三十六景　信州　諏訪湖
前北斎為一筆

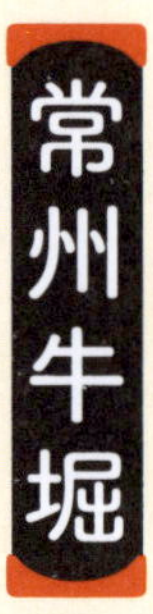

4

Ushibori in Hitachi Province

Joshu Ushibori

A large boat cuts diagonally across the foreground, dividing the print into two. While its bow rises to the left, the stern hides behind a rocky hill as if it were an appendage. The boat's size make the houses in the distance along with Fuji appear tiny in comparison. On the boat, whose mast is lowered, a man empties water from a vase after having just washed some rice; other people look around inside. At the back, we see sacks of cargo and folded reed mats. Hokusai gives us a glimpse into the lives of these boatmen and carefully portrays the boat inside and out.

The water in the scene blends into the ground and flows into the clouds and sky as if they were all made of the same substance. On the left, two herons fly away in the same direction as the boat's bow. Silence seems to reign supreme. Fuji emerges in the background behind a field of still reeds, untouched by wind; we are in winter. The exclusive use of blue tones creates a serene but lively landscape, perfect for fishermen going about their daily routine.

The boat sits in a swampy area near the port of Ushibori on Lake Kasumigaura, the second-largest lake in Japan. Located northeast of Tokyo, it is in today's Ibaraki Prefecture. Ushibori is quite far from Mount Fuji and is probably the easternmost region from which the mountain can still be seen.

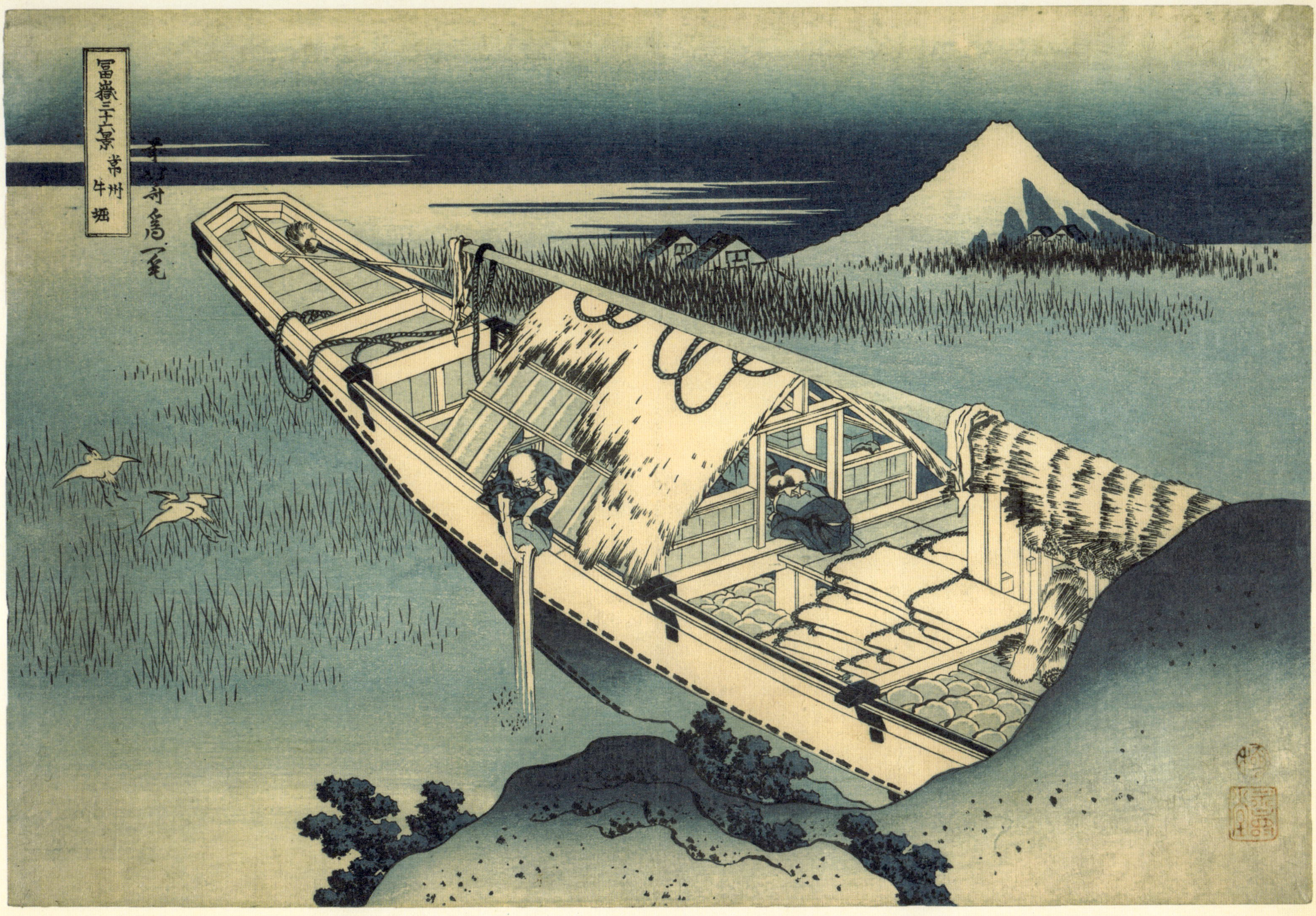

冨嶽三十六景　常州牛堀
前北斎為一筆

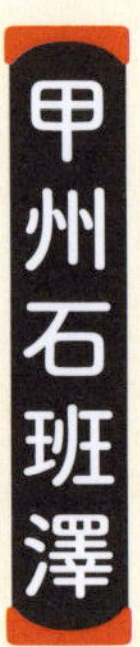

5

Kajikazawa in Kai Province

Koshu Kajikazawa

This is one of the most successful and evocative prints in the Fuji series. In its simple composition, Hokusai unites the strength of nature with the fragility—but also the endurance—of man. A fisherman, his son seated behind him with a fishing basket, holds outstretched fishing lines that are cast into the water. Despite the tension and effort involved, the man seems relaxed. Beyond the roar of the waves, a dense fog bank conceals much of Fuji, leaving only its summit visible.

The composition is organized according to a simple geometric principle: the repetition of similar shapes in different positions. The silhouette of Fuji is counterposed between the threads stretched out to one side and by the contours of the rocky cliff on which the figures stand.

The bent man's figure is juxtaposed with the peak of the mountain. Even the waves, reminiscent of the movements of the *The Great Wave* (#16), mirror the triangular shape of the mountain.

The first impression of this print featured only blue tones. Subsequent versions added green to the rock and brown to the figures, diminishing the sense of continuity between the human and natural elements that makes the whole so powerful.

Kajikazawa is located in Yamanashi Prefecture, about halfway between Tokyo and Nagoya. From the image it looks as if the man is fishing in the open sea, but the location is actually inland. It is probably the point at which the Kamanashi and Fuefuki rivers flow into the Fuji River.

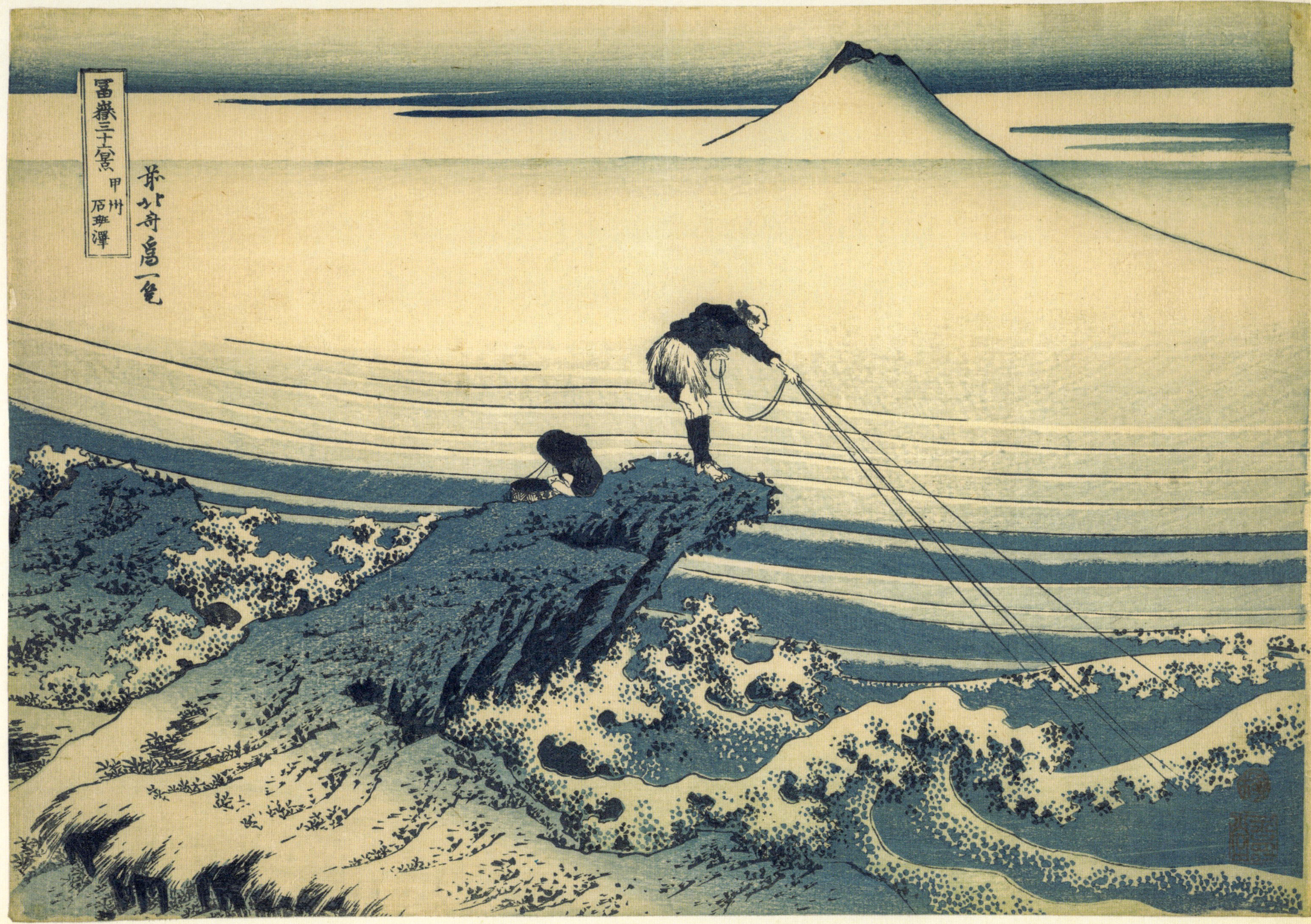
冨嶽三十六景　甲州石班澤
北齋改爲一筆

6

In the Mountains of Totomi Province

Totomi Sanchu

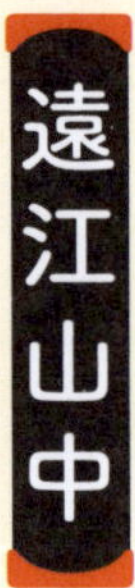

This is one of the most outstanding prints in the series in terms of composition. In the foreground, a man is busy sawing a thick log, presumably together with members of his family. He saws it from above while another man does the same from below; a third, seated, is repairing a saw, while in the center of the scene another worker, sitting cross-legged, guards a fire that radiates dark smoke. Under the pillars supporting the large log, a woman carries a child on her shoulders as she addresses the seated man; the child looks away, his gaze fixated on Fuji.

The volcano is framed by the pillars supporting the wood, circled by a line of white clouds. Gray smoke from the fire, meant to mirror the clouds, is only partially visible in the print.

Despite a limited color palette, Hokusai shows us different aspects of labor in a compositional frame rich with diverse elements—wood, earth, clouds, smoke. He adopted a gradation technique called *bokashi* used frequently by engravers to capture the depth of rivers and the vastness of the sky. The image is dominated by a series of triangular shapes, not only in the pillars and the trunk, but also in the inverted triangles created by the log, the smoke and the hill on the right side.

The scene is probably set in the mountainous area of Shizuoka between the Tenryu and Oi rivers.

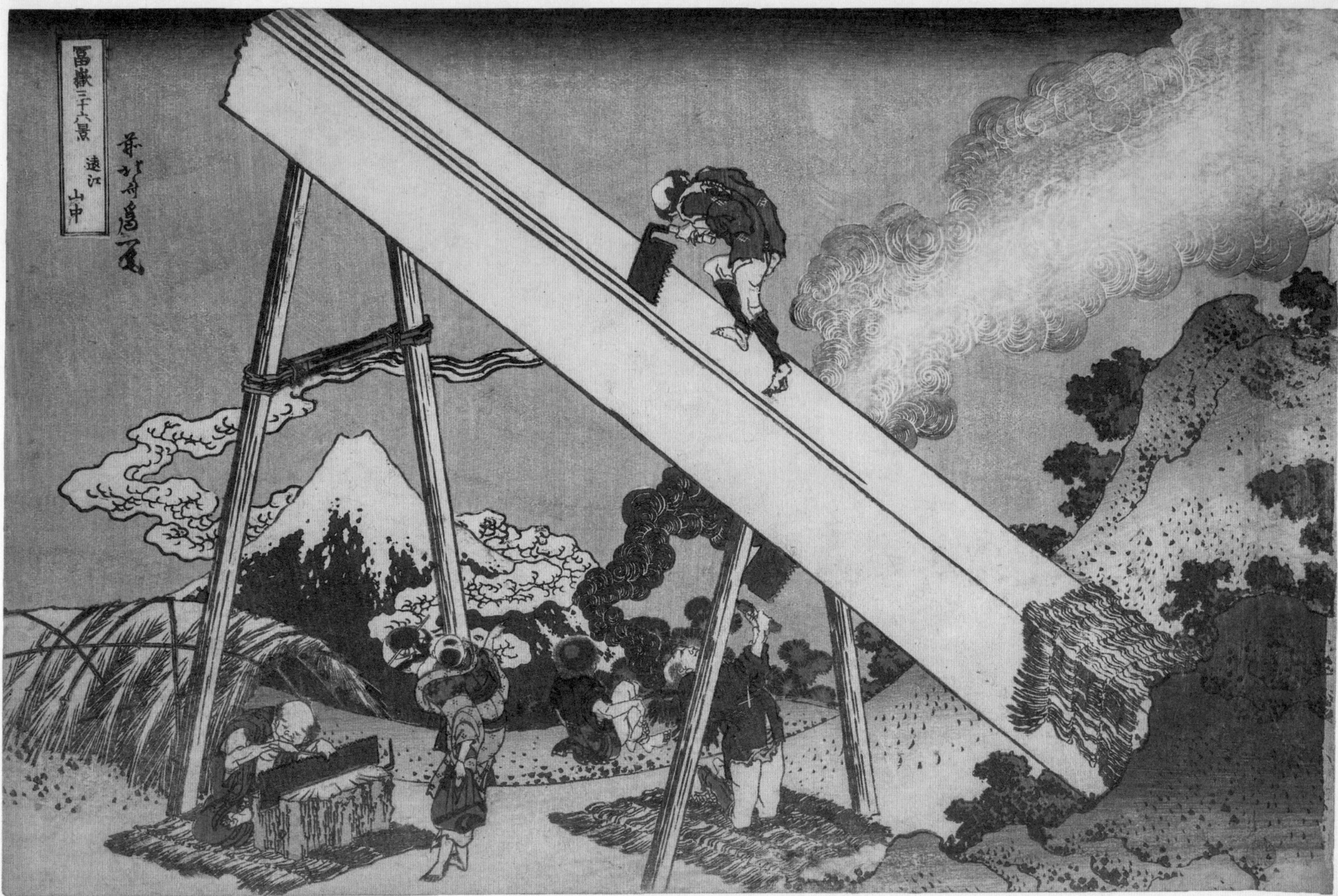

冨嶽三十六景　遠江　山中
前北斎為一筆

7

Umezawa Manor in Sagami Province

Soshu Umezawa Hidari

For this print, Hokusai used gentle tones of blue, light green and pale pink. Blue is also used for the outlines in place of black. Both the sky and the snow on top of the volcano have been rendered with the shaded *bokashi* technique, creating a mirror effect. Surrounded by banks of fog, the sacred mountain rises majestically above the rolling green hills below. The ensemble evokes a sense of great tranquility and timeless peace.

Hokusai links Fuji to the crane, a symbol of longevity and good luck. In Japan, the combination is auspicious and rich in meaning. Five birds are on the ground and two in flight. The latter, flying parallel to the line of the mountain, give Fuji a sense of depth and distance. Shades of peach in the clouds and low mist all around the scene suggest that dawn is not far away.

Sagami is now located in Kanagawa Prefecture, southwest of Tokyo. The last character in the print's title, *hidari* 左 ("left"), appears to be a misprint. In its place should be the character *sho* 庄 or *zai* 在, for "estate" or "manor."

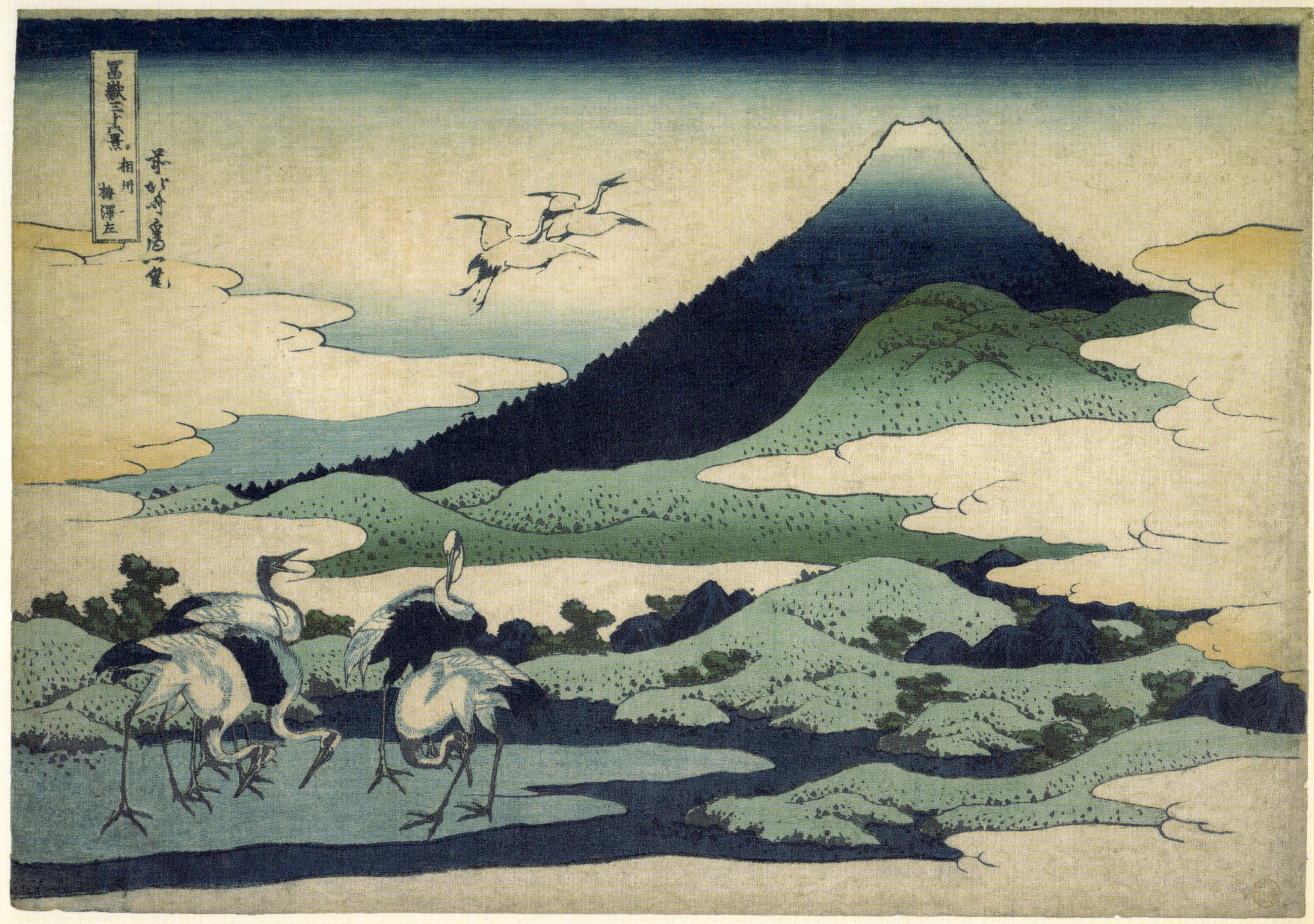

8

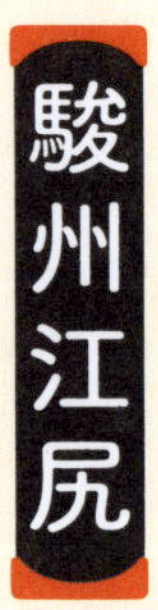

Ejiri in Suruga Province

Sunshu Ejiri

Pilgrims are surprised by a strong wind when walking through the rice fields in Ejiri. The invisible wind is ingeniously represented by the straw hats and sheets of paper that flutter away from the woman's bag on the left, as well as the contorted bodies and trees fighting to resist its force. A hat can be seen flying away on the right-hand side of the print.

Ejiri was a post station on the Tokaido road in today's Shizuoka Prefecture, which ran through Shimizu Port, southeast of Mount Fuji. The town was famous for the beautiful Miho no Matsubara Pine Grove, a popular subject of art and poetry since the Muromachi period (1392–1573). However, Hokusai chose to depict a lesser-known spot in Ejiri—where an elevated path bends around a swamp—and made a gust of wind the protagonist of the scene.

Sudden flurries of wind often blow at the foot of Mount Fuji. Although the mountain is barely outlined, and as white as the surrounding sky, its figure exudes a sense of stability and solidness amidst the bustling winds.

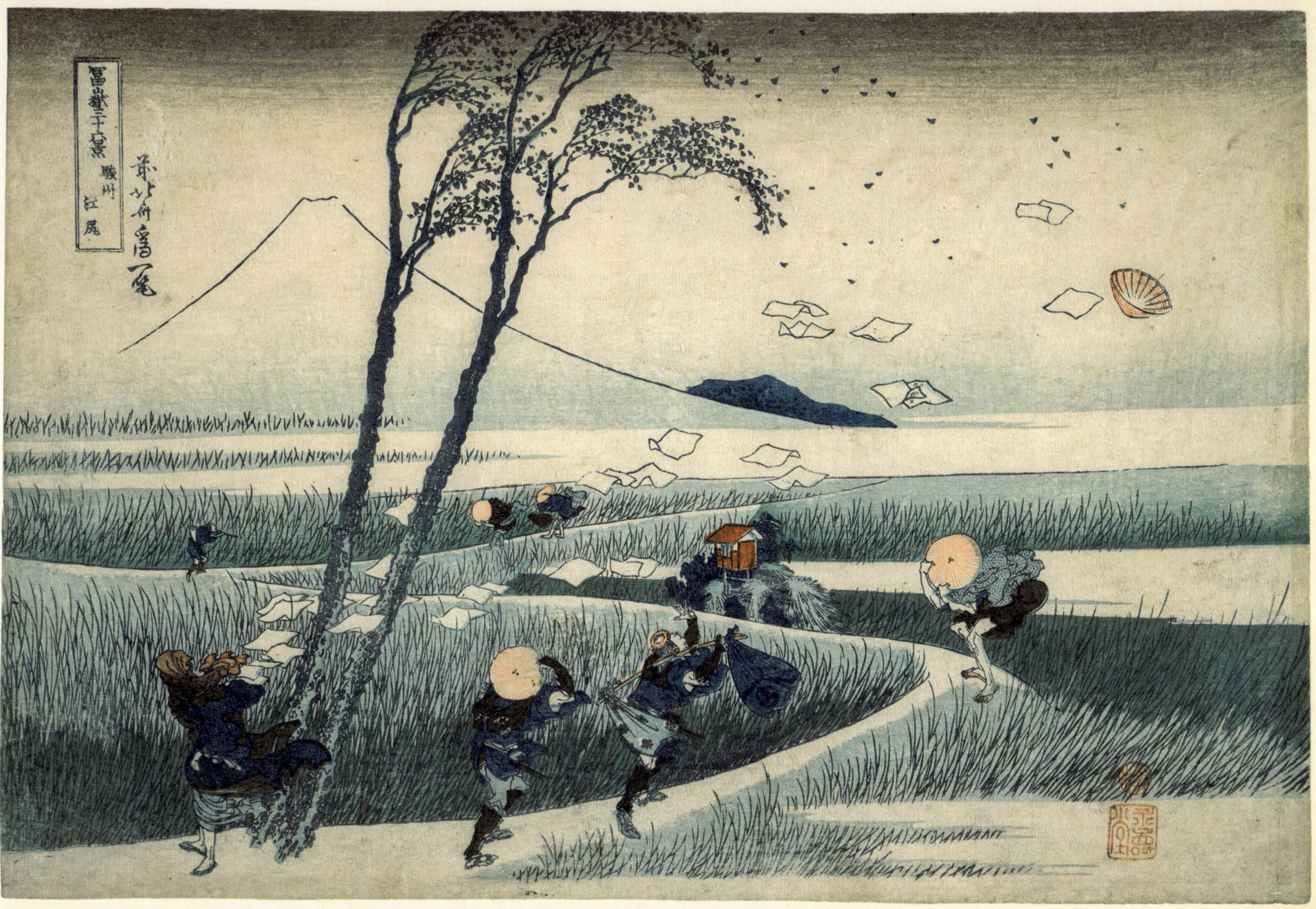

冨嶽三十六景 駿州江尻
前北斎為一筆

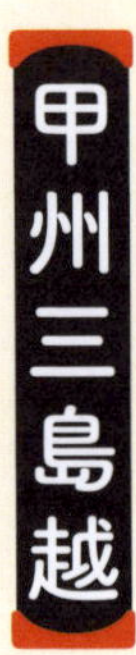

9

Mishima Pass in Kai Province

Koshu Mishima Goe

Having just completed their trek, a group of pilgrims exult a hundred-year-old cedar tree by wrapping their arms around its circumference. Meanwhile, other fellow travelers continue down the path on the right; another man can be seen resting on the left as he smokes his pipe.

With only its massive trunk and low-hanging leaves visible, the tree exudes a majestic, imposing presence that dwarfs that of Fuji. The travelers appear as playful children; they celebrate nature with a festive spirit, free—even if only momentarily—from the cares of daily life. Hokusai succeeds in depicting the human condition even in such a limited and nature-centric portrait, a testament to his love for humanity.

Once again, the artist uses geometry to frame the scene in an original way. The left slope of Fuji runs parallel to a stray branch hanging from the tree, creating diagonal symmetry. The natural elements exhibit a masterful use of *bokashi* shading. Fuji is rendered in three colors that range from the charcoal gray base to a white mid-layer to the dark blue of the summit. The use of few colors graces the work with a simple elegance.

The exact location of the Mishima Pass is uncertain. It could be the Kagosaka Pass, or this print could be one of the views that was imagined by Hokusai.

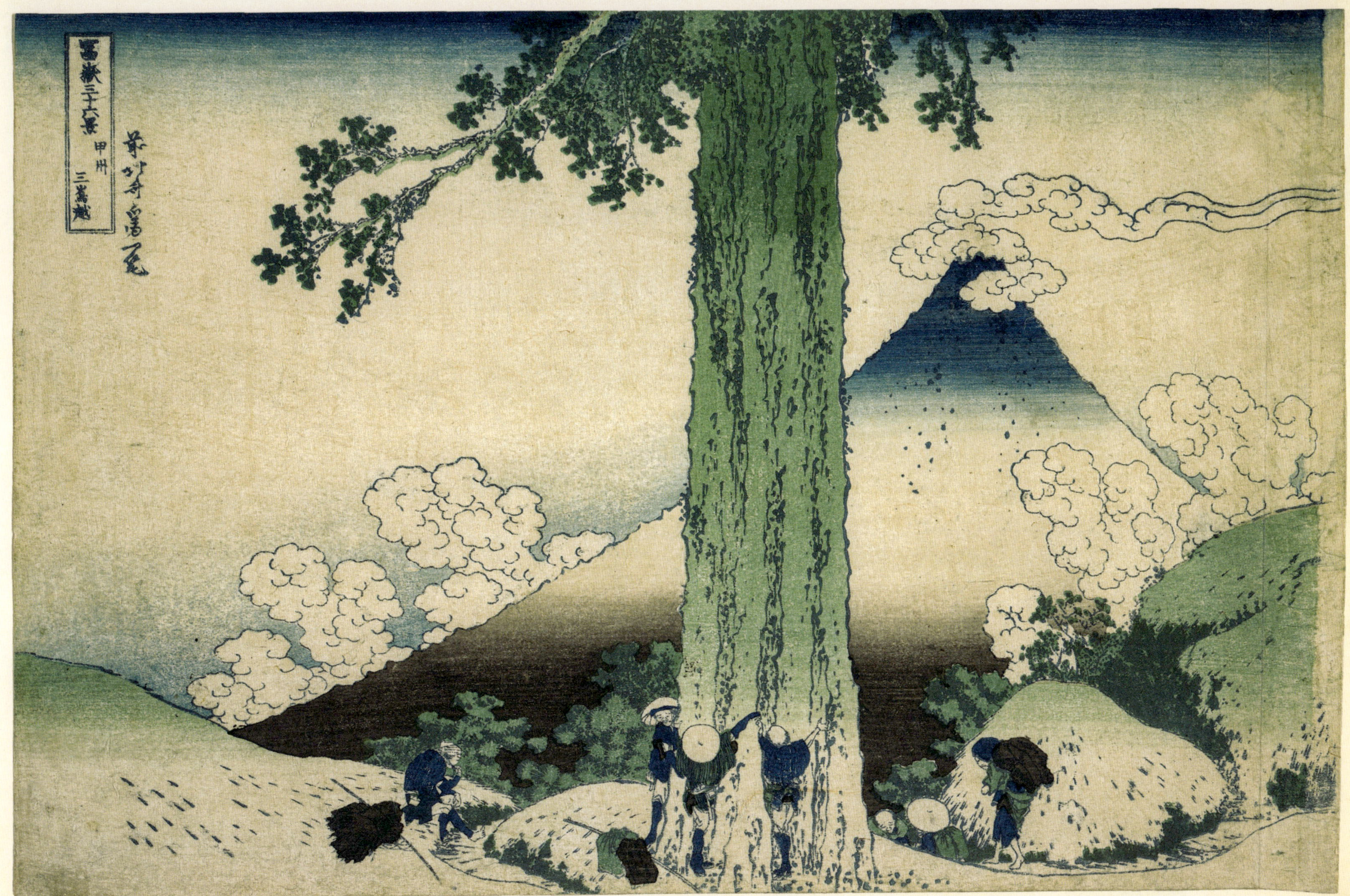
冨嶽三十六景
甲州
三嶌越
北斎改爲一筆

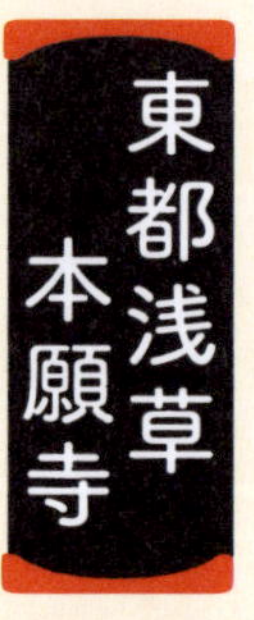

10

Honganji at Asakusa in Edo

Toto Asakusa Honganji

The Honganji was a large Buddhist temple built in 1657 in the Asakusa district in Edo, the most populous part of the city. Hokusai gives us an extreme close-up of the roof's triangular pediment. From here, we gain a vantage point above the roof and the clouds.

Fuji's slopes can be seen rising above the clouds in the distance, its shape imitated in the contours of the temple and the small houses below—where workers can be seen making repairs on the roof. The exaggerated yet detailed postures of these men recall Hokusai's studies of form and movement, which culminated in the publication of his *Manga* sketchbooks. The string of a phoenix-shaped kite, running parallel to the roof's slope, seems to point toward Fuji.

A mythical animal, the phoenix is one of the four celestial guardians associated with the cardinal points. According to myth, it manifests in times of prosperity and symbolizes rebirth, peace and the absence of chaos. This print is set at the beginning of the year. The Japanese loved to fly kites at this time and the windy winter days were ideal for doing so. The presence of the phoenix, alongside human activities of work and play, help amplify the symbolic value of Fuji.

The tall wooden scaffold on the left side of the print—a lookout point for firemen—balances out the domineering presence of the temple roof on the right-hand side.

This is one of the prints made almost entirely of shades of Prussian blue. In some versions, the kite and a few clouds are colored in orange.

A similar composition can be found in print #26—*Mitsui Shop at Surugacho in Edo (Edo surugacho mitsui mise ryakuzu)*, which also features a roof in the foreground, a kite and a balancing of architectural elements between the right and left sides of the print.

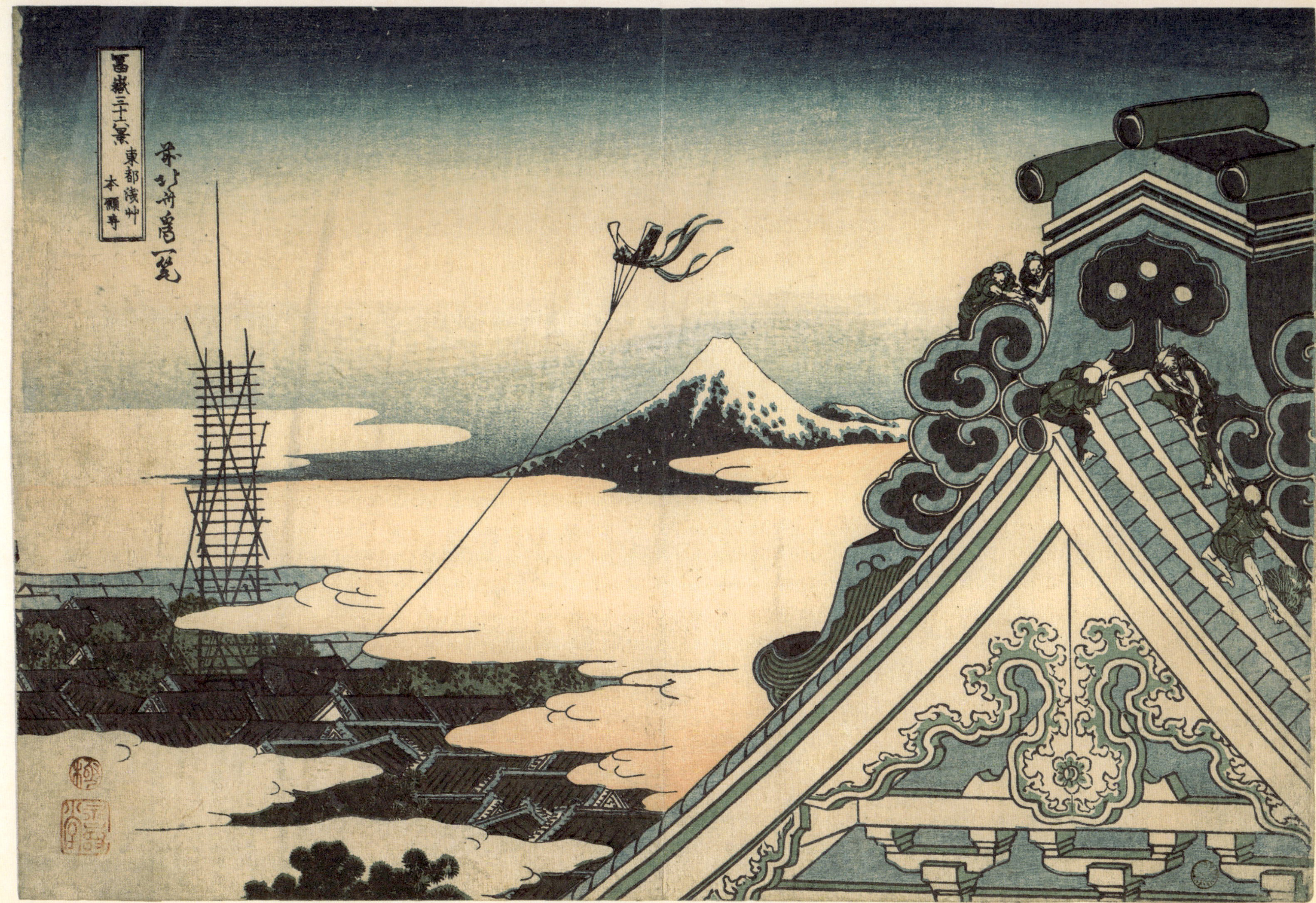
冨嶽三十六景
東都淺草
本願寺
前北齋爲一筆

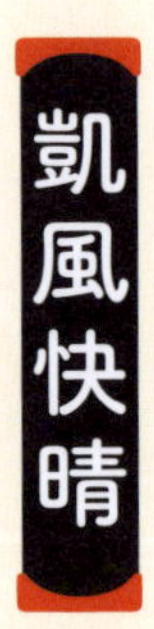

11

South Wind, Clear Sky aka "Red Fuji"

Gaifu Kaisei

This is an unusual Fuji with little snow. The work is defined by three main colors—red, blue and green—and a compositional simplicity bordering on abstraction; perspective is absent and human elements are nowhere to be found. The red of the rock is interrupted by patches of melting snow, the blue of the sky streaked by morning clouds and the green of the mountain's base is dotted with small trees that appear like tiny cones. The words "South Wind" in the title, *gaifu*, refers to the light southern breeze that comes in during the summer months when there is little snow on the summit. From then until autumn, Fuji takes on a reddish hue in the early morning. Indeed, the best time to admire red Fuji is late into the summer when the weak winds create rippled, "cirrocumulus" clouds that make for easy viewing. At the foot of the mountain, the small trees are rendered with obvious simplicity to amplify the grandeur of Fuji.

In China, the "south wind" arrives at the beginning of summer and is believed to confer longevity on all living beings. Hokusai here compares Mount Fuji to the legendary Mount Horai in Chinese mythology. An island of eternal youth, it was a place free of human worry and a popular subject in the arts—legend held that one could only reach it by flying on the back of a crane.

Mount Fuji is not actually this steep in reality. Even though its slopes are less than 45°, Hokusai exaggerated the angles for dramatic effect. In other prints, the artist immerses us in the tumultuous struggle between the human spirit and the forces of nature; here, nature is depicted as majestic, beautiful and powerless, but also peaceful and solitary.

This print and #12 *Storm Below Mount Fuji* (*Sanka haku*) are the only ones in the series without any indication of the perspective from which the mountain is depicted. Without any other useful references in the image, it is difficult to identify a location. Some suggest that the spot to recapture this view can be found in the vicinity of Lake Kawaguchi in Yamanashi Prefecture.

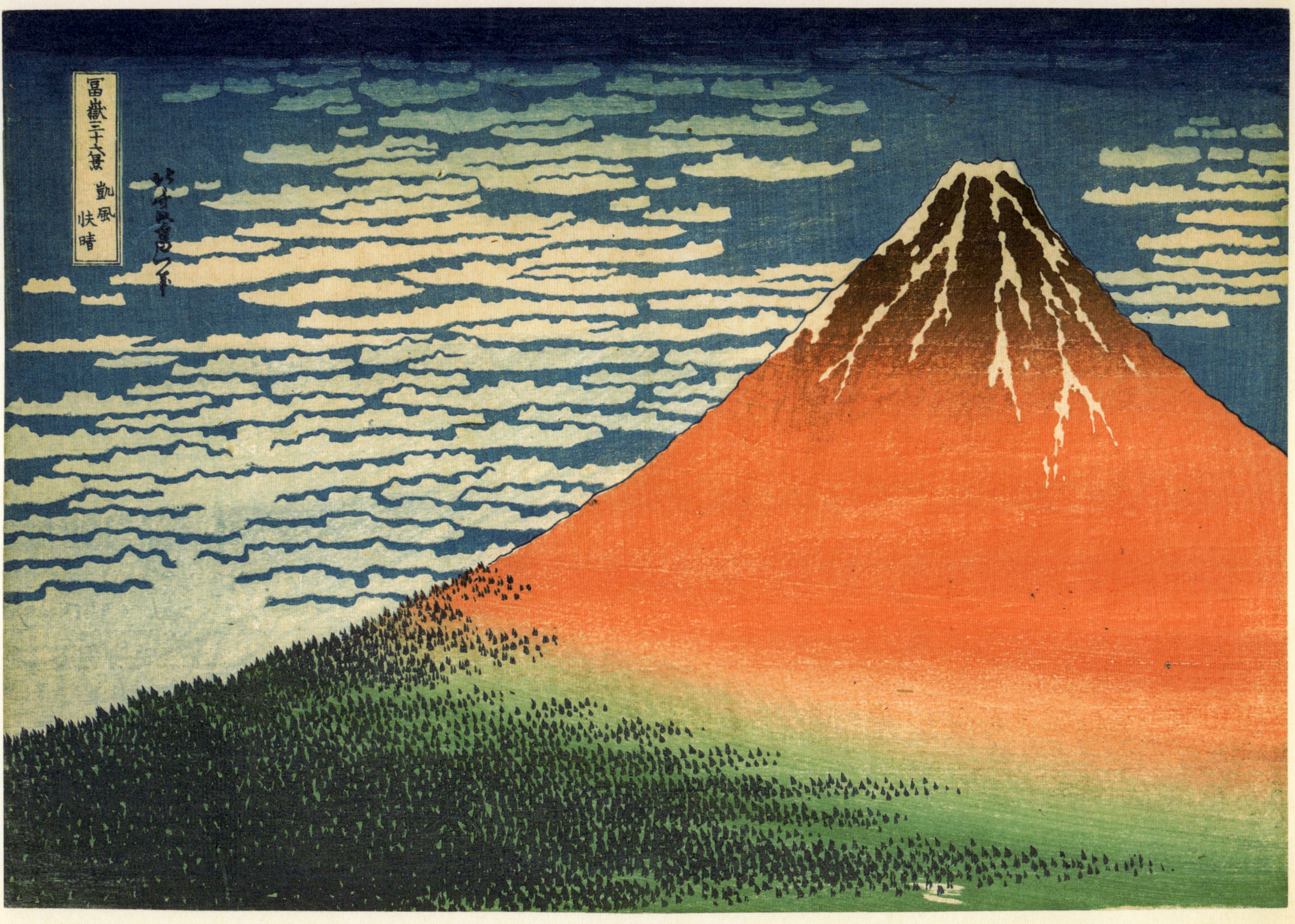
冨嶽三十六景　凱風快晴
北斎改爲一筆

In Hokusai's subsequent series, *One Hundred Views of Mount Fuji* (*Fugaku hyakkei,* 1834–1835), the print at right shows a composition very similar to the one on the next page—#64 *Fuji in Deep Snow* (*Shinsetsu no Fuji*). The season is a different one, the top of the mountain is snow-capped and the base is speckled, as is the sky, with snow falling on the pilgrims on the road below.

The addition of these characters who brave the snow alongside Fuji introduces the theme of human struggle and establishes a bond between nature and humans. The snowflakes in the upper part of the print find their mirror image in the black footprints left by the pilgrims in the lower part.

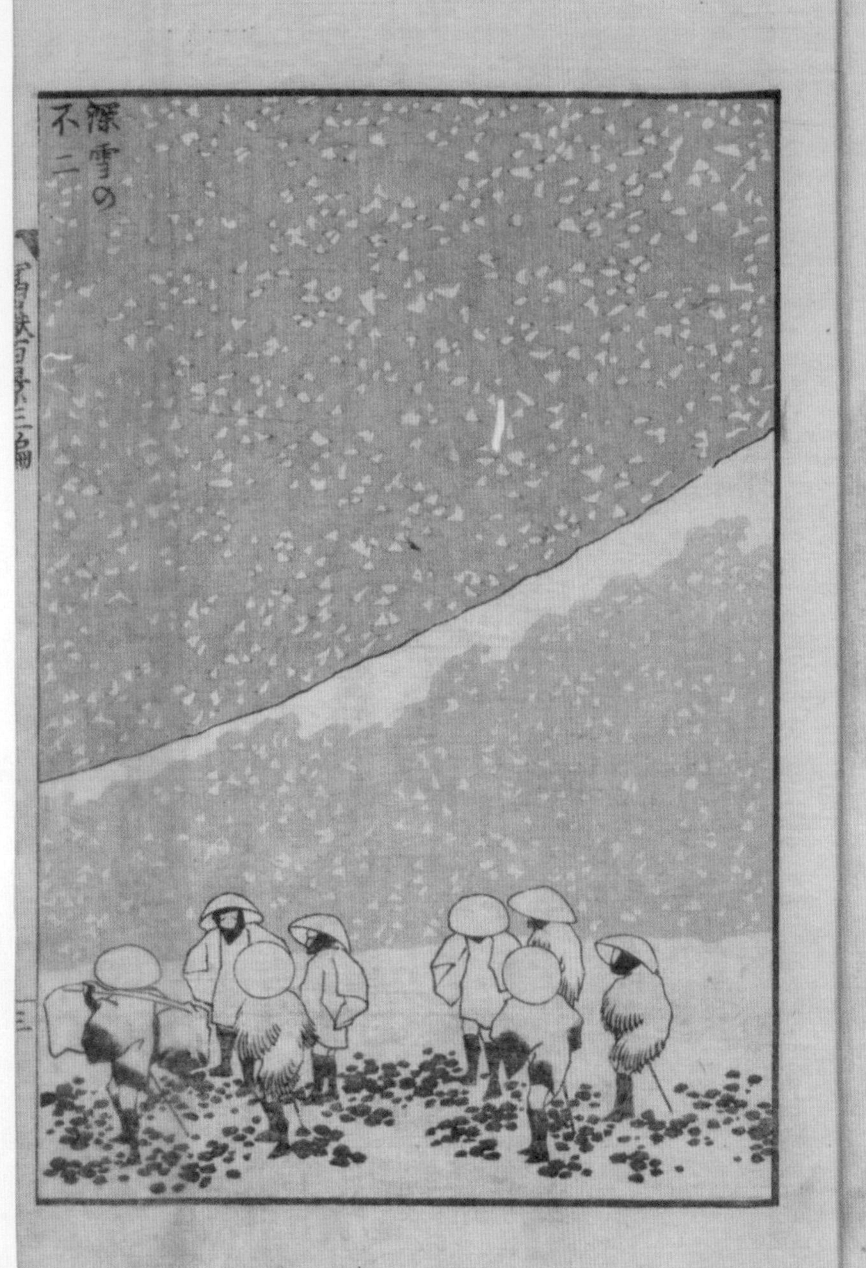

深雪の不二
富嶽百景三編

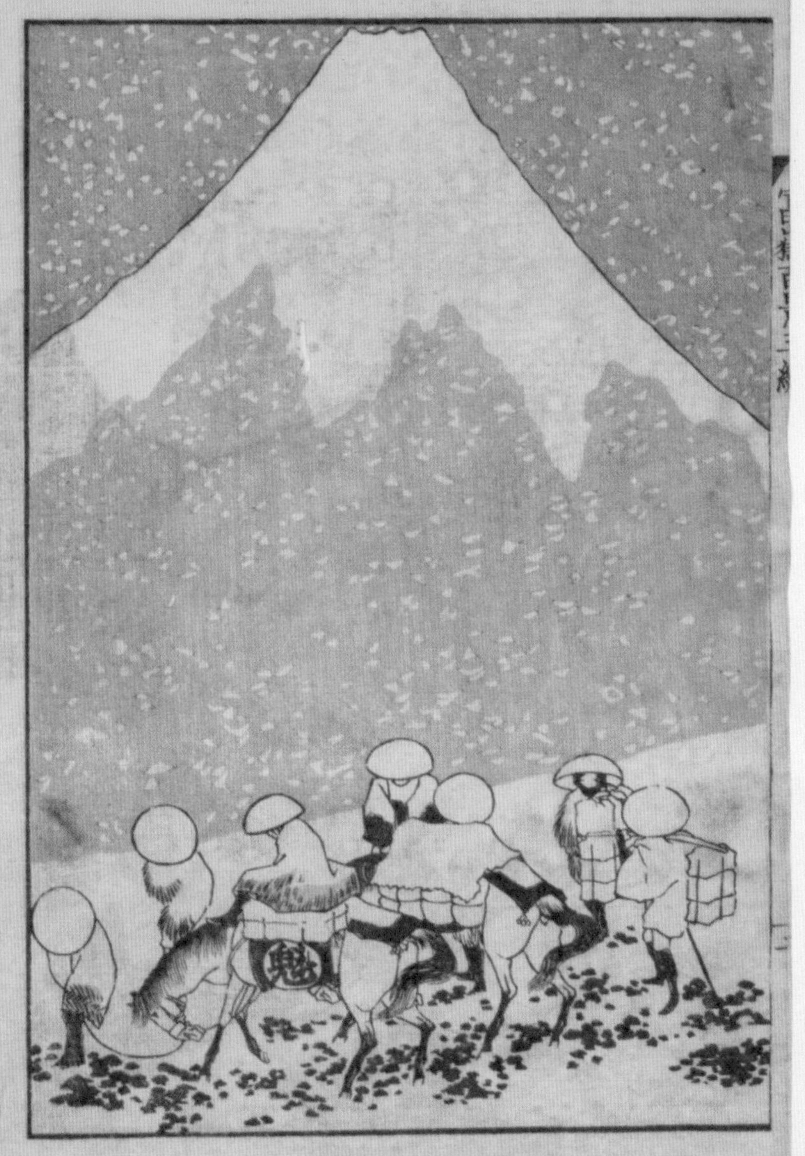

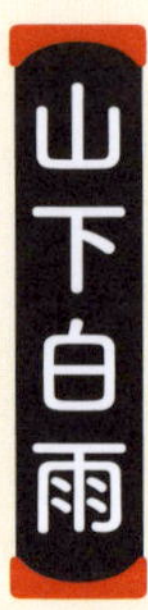

12

Storm Below Mount Fuji aka "Black Fuji"

Sanka Haku

This is the third most famous work in the series behind #16 and #11. The composition and perspective are similar to those of the previous print. The viewing point is clearly higher up, however—as in *Red Fuji*—the location is obfuscated. Hokusai thus probably recreated this aerial perspective from his imagination.

Moreover, the peace of the previous print is disturbed here by another natural element: lightning. But it is caught at the foot of the mountain, not above, as if to affirm that Fuji is the greater force of nature in Japan. The clouds in the background are soft and serene, but toward the bottom the colors turn somber as the base of the mountain, almost black, is torn asunder by the lightning bolts. The clashing tones give the composition a striking and dramatic flair absent in *Red Fuji*.

The storm that gives the work its name is not visible. In fact, the summit of the mountain (12,389 feet/3776 meters) is at such a high elevation that it never rains there. Showers therefore only occur lower down; the lightning and striking color scheme are enough to imply their presence. Hokusai demonstrates here his masterful ability to represent things in an indirect way.

Fuji, eternal and unchanging, is untouched by the vicissitudes of men who are likely seeking shelter from the storm down below. The work finds harmony in the internal conflicts between light and dark, movement and stillness, and also in juxtaposition to *Red Fuji*.

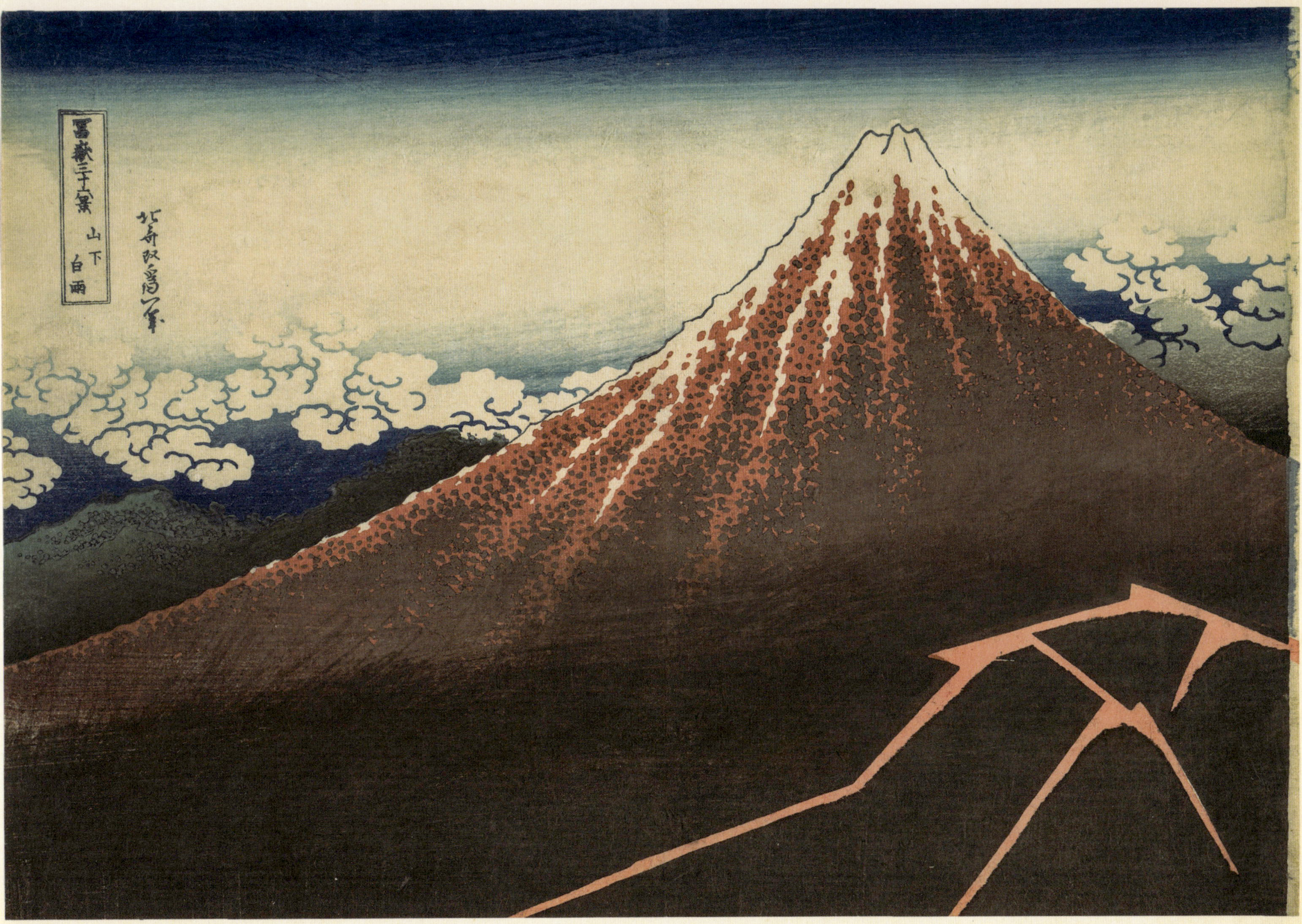
冨嶽三十六景
山下白雨
北斎改為一筆

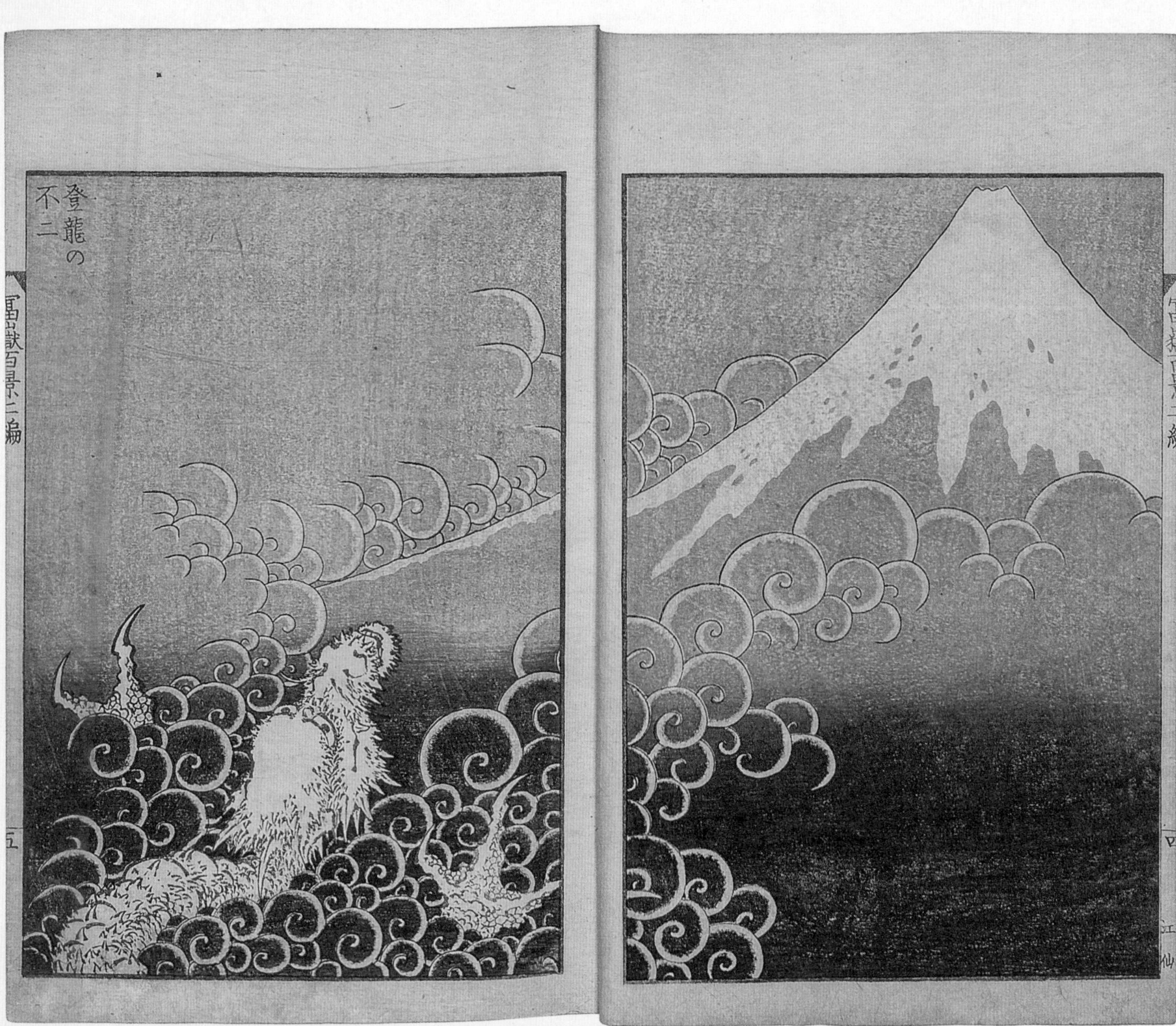

In his later series, *One Hundred Views of Mount Fuji* (*Fugaku hyakkei*), Hokusai would include a print similar to *Black Fuji*—#36 *The Ascent (of the Dragon) to Fuji* (*Toryu no Fuji*). But at the foot of the mountain, twirling in the clouds, he added a dragon, another of his much-loved subjects.

There is another print that recalls the composition of *Black Fuji* where lightning strikes the mountain. But this time it hits a village already terrorized by the wind, where small figures seek shelter from the bad weather—print #52 *Fuji in a Thunderstorm* (*Yudachi no Fuji*), see image on the right. Lightning rips through the sky on both sides of the print. The presence of man accentuates the stakes of the drama.

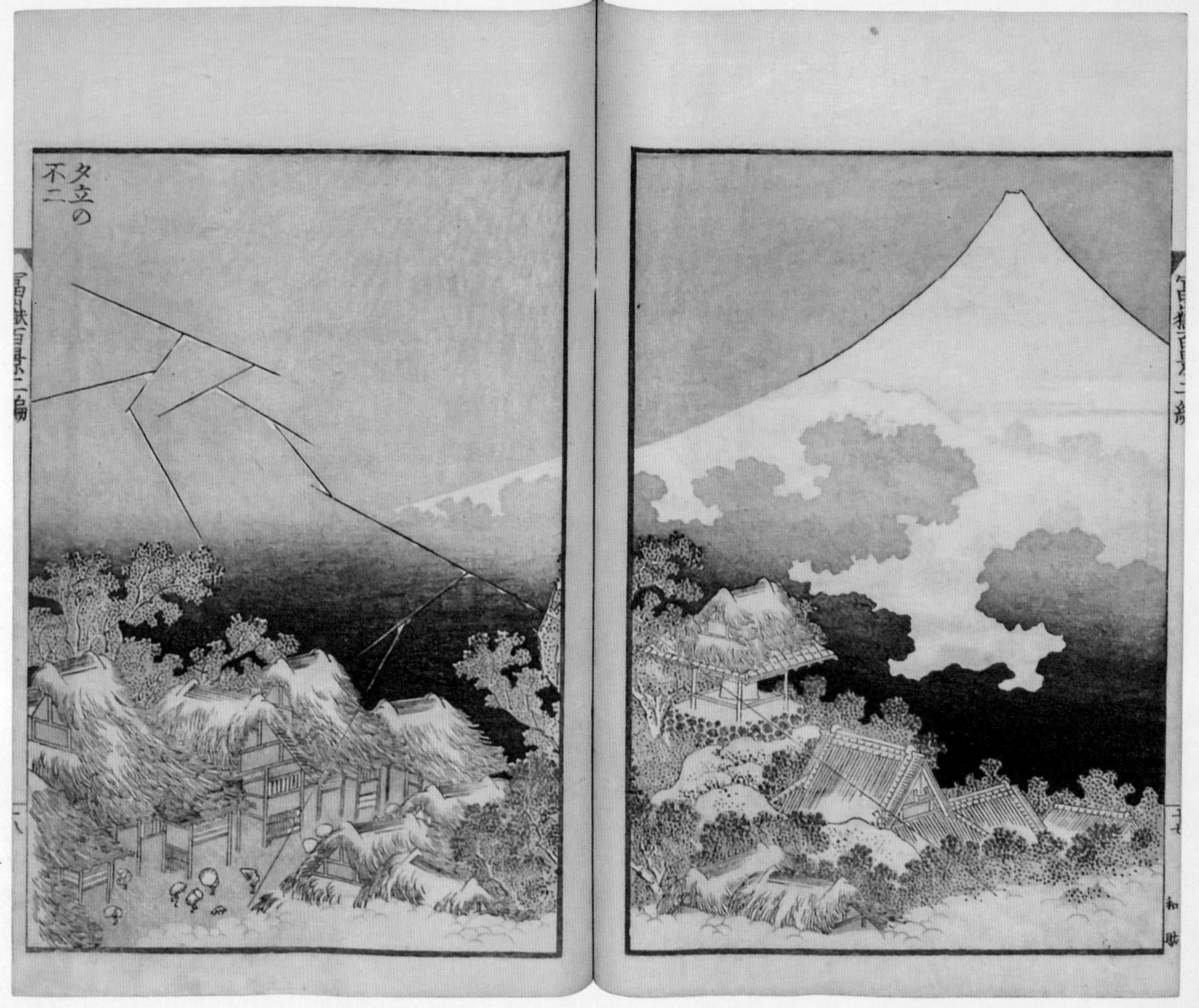

13

Senju in Musashi Province

Bushu Senju

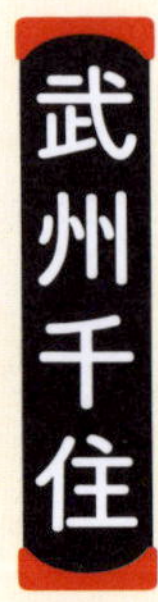

Two fishermen and a farmer look up to admire Fuji, as if mesmerized for the first time by its beauty and grandeur. The mountain is partially obscured by a wooden structure, most likely posts erected for the construction of a house. They do not detract from its splendor, but rather emphasize its beauty.

The filtering of perspective through another object evokes *kaimami*, a literary motif where the act of observation—usually peeping at women through the sliding panels of traditional Japanese dwellings—leads one to fall in love. The practice was widespread among nobles from the Heian era onwards, particularly in pleasure quarters where courtesans were admired through wooden slits and eventually selected.

The horse's downward arch, with the high-saddle between its reclined back and lowered head, recall the convex shape of the mountain. The fishing pole of the man on the left and the white lines protruding from the step seem pointed towards the distant, snow-covered Fuji. The horse is laden with grass-filled bags. At the bottom, attached to its rope, hangs a turtle, an emblem of long life and good fortune. Meaning "prosperous mountain," Fuji's name conveys the same symbolism as that of the turtle. The lines of rope create a "V" as if inverting the shape of Fuji.

Senju was the first post town on the Nikko Kaido and Oshu Kaido, two of the five major Gokaido ("Five Routes") that ran through Japan, and was known as one of the four most important post stations in Edo times. Musashi was a province that consists of the present prefectures of Tokyo, parts of Saitama and Kanagawa, Kawasaki and Yokohama.

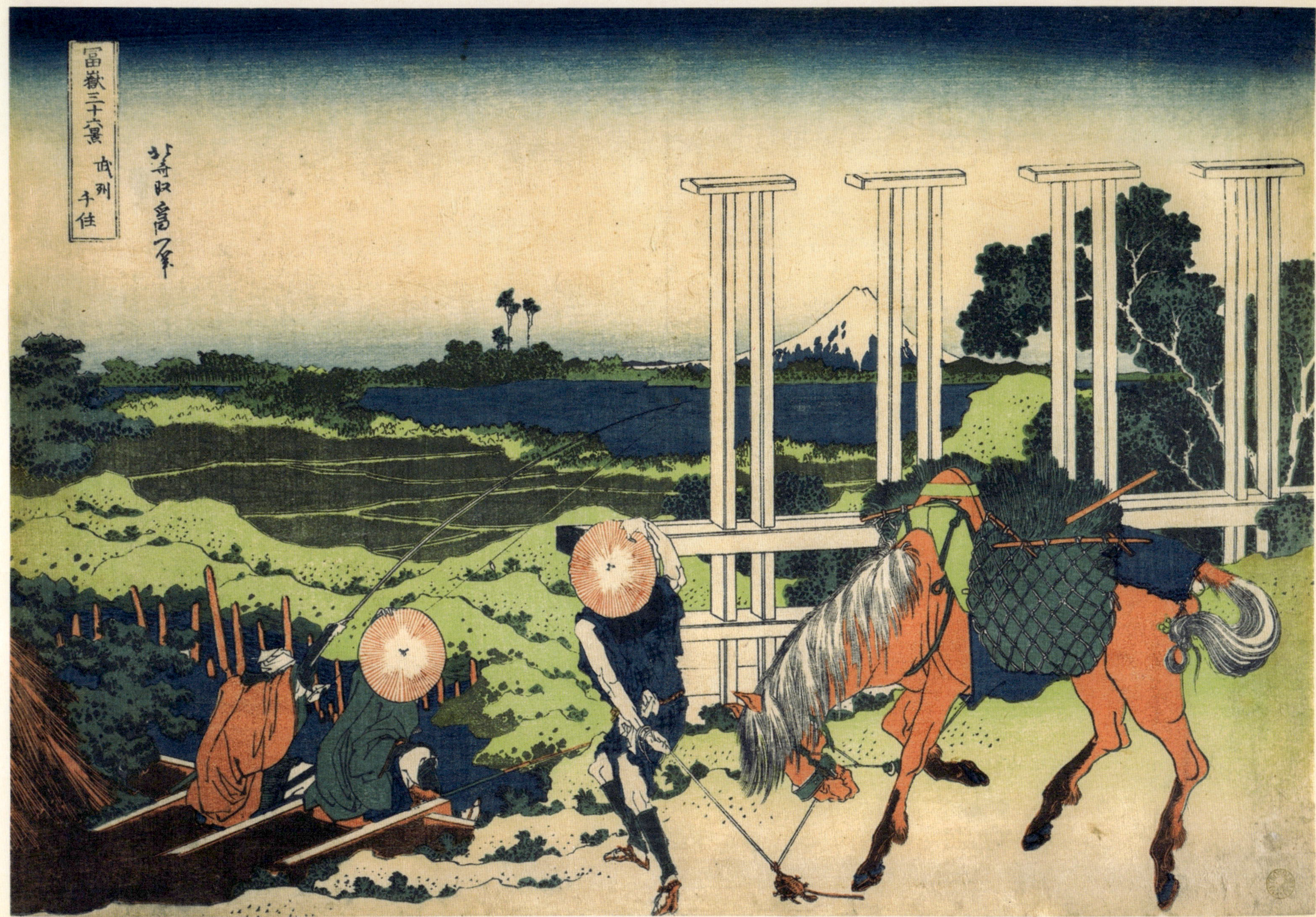
冨嶽三十六景　武列　千住
前北斎為一筆

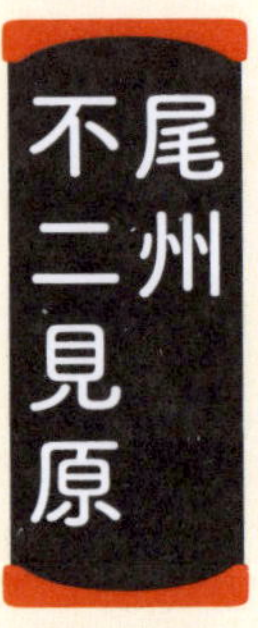

14

Fujimigahara in Owari Province

Bishu Fujimigahara

This is the first print in the series that conveys a human's existence so intimately. Framed inside a perfect circle—a large barrel being constructed by a lone man in the scene—Fuji is tucked away beyond a dense forest. The cone of the summit enters into perfect, geometric harmony with the circle and the paddy fields in the background.

The man is dressed in light clothing, bare-chested, a *furoshiki* on his head and simple *zori* slippers on his feet; cluttered around him are various tools of his trade. Among the many prints in the series that depict artisans, this one is considered a masterpiece.

Visual guides direct our gaze to toward Fuji: the framing lines etched into the ground and the cane resting on the ground to the left. The craftsman, though seemingly indifferent, cannot help but bask in the majestic presence behind him.

The combination of the sacred mountain and the worker lends a religious tone to the man's life and work. Owari province (Owari no Kuni 尾張国), abbreviated as Bishu, corresponded to the west of present-day Aichi Prefecture, east of Nagoya. Fujimigahara was a well-known scenic spot which housed pleasure quarters and samurai residences.

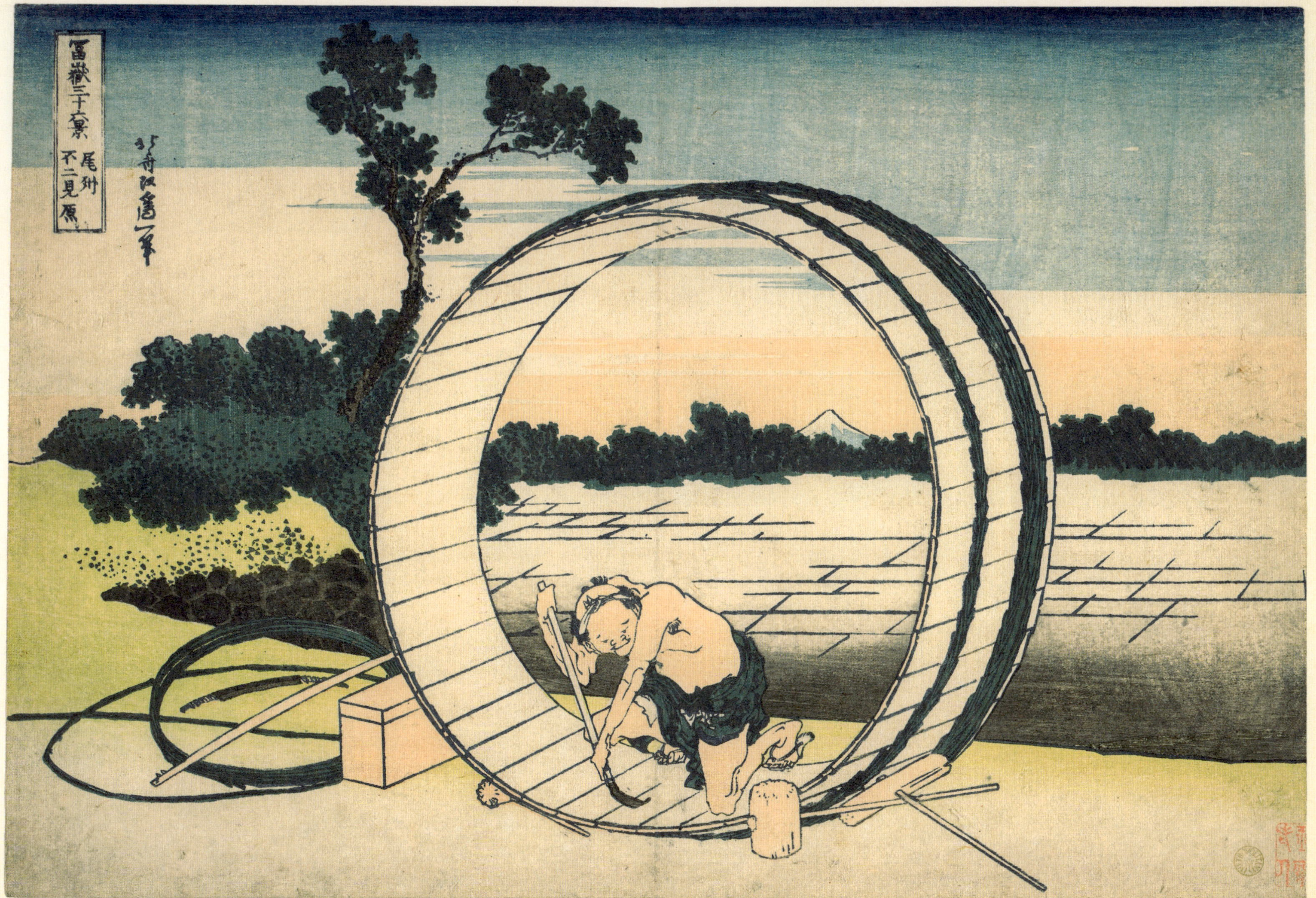

冨嶽三十六景　尾州不二見原
北斎改爲一筆

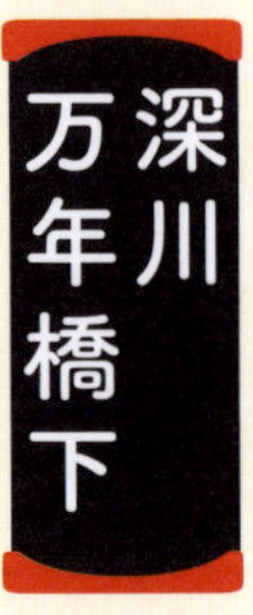

15

Under the Mannen Bridge at Fukagawa

Fukagawa Mannenbashi Shita

The Mannen ("Ten Thousand Years") Bridge dominates the composition and frames Fuji in the distance. The perspective lines of the composition converge with the prows of the boats, setting the stage for intense human activity.

Fukagawa is a district of Tokyo in the Koto area and is where Hokusai lived for some time in his later years. The bridge still exists, but no longer in its original form. It crosses the estuary where the Onagi River flows into the Sumida, east of Tokyo. The place was known for its view of Mount Fuji in the distance behind the Sumida River, however today it is blocked by tall buildings.

The bridge was built so high because of its long span. The entire area of Fukagawa was at an altitude below sea level, so both sides of the bridge were raised and walled up in case of flooding. Hokusai notably highlights the curvature of this *taikobashi* ("drum bridge").

The print shows some people crossing the bridge, others working on boats or catching fish. The Onagi River was an artificial waterway built by Shogun Tokugawa Ieyasu to transport salt and various other goods between Chiba and Edo. On the river, a man can be seen fishing alone. The contrast between his solitary, silent activity and the hustle on the bridge masterfully renders the human condition with diversity and charm. Fuji sits at the back next to what appears to be a watchtower—as in other prints from the series, its quiet presence instills a sense of time that is simultaneously passing yet eternal, an aura of presentness that fuses together all the elements in the scene.

Above, the sky's gradients have been rendered with *bokashi*. A large blue umbrella in the middle of the bridge recalls the sun and creates a point of balance with the boat below. Hokusai uses Western style perspective here, although not entirely consistently.

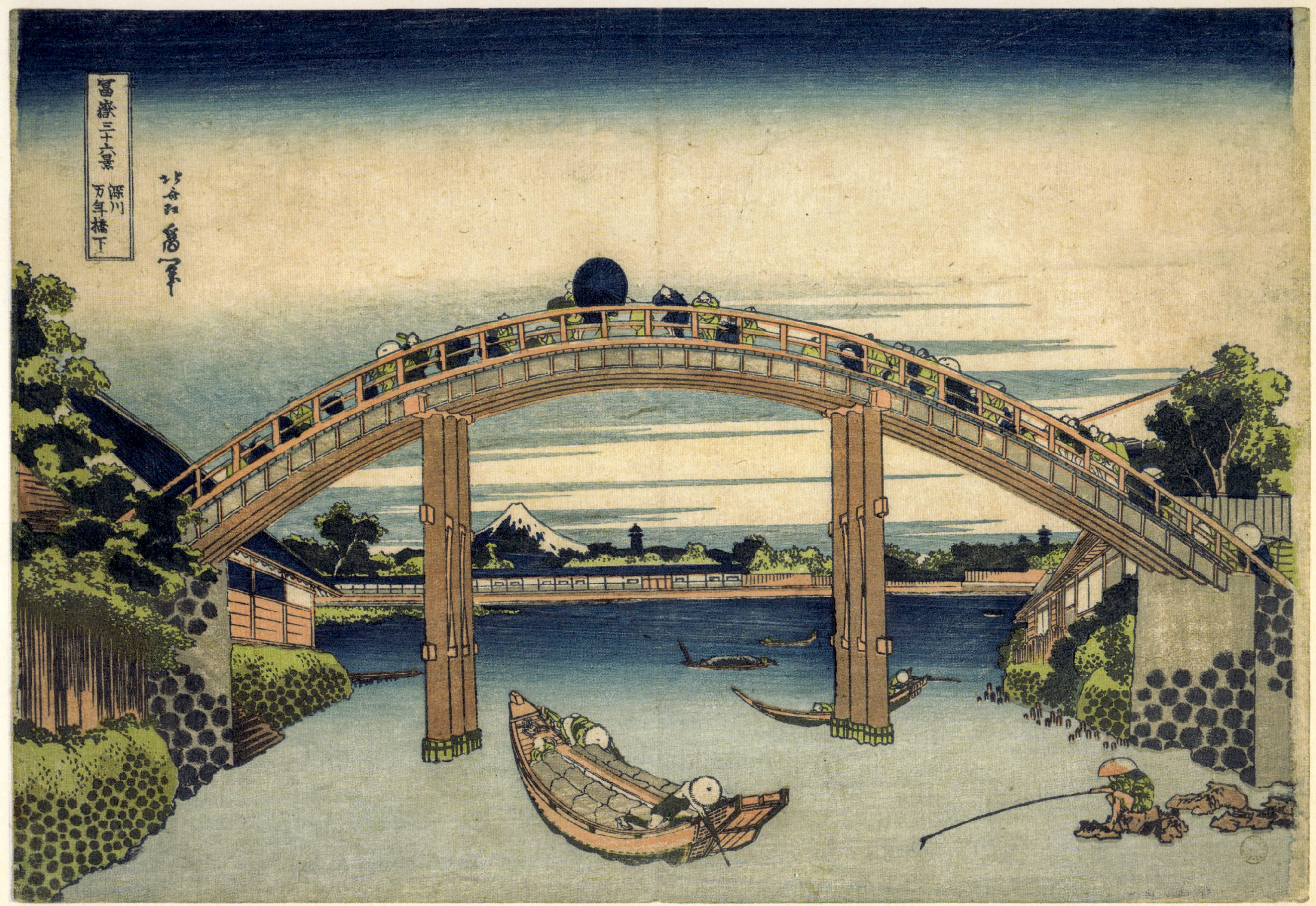

冨嶽三十六景
深川
万年橋下
北斎
画筆

Under the Wave Off Kanagawa
aka "The Great Wave"
Kanagawa Oki Nami Ura

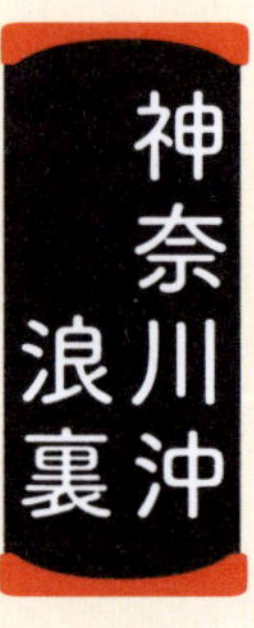

This is Hokusai's greatest masterpiece and probably the most recognized work of Japanese art in the world. The image depicts a view of Mount Fuji off the coast of present-day Yokohama in Kanagawa Prefecture, south of Tokyo. In the foreground, three boats carrying several men struggle against the threatening waves, fighting to not get swept away.

Throughout his life Hokusai experimented with different methods of rendering numerous expressions of waves. In this instance, he used alternating hues of deep blue and sky blue to create a sense of depth and capture the motion of the foam. The small crests on the crashing waves resemble the claws of a dragon, another of the artist's favorite subjects. Below the large wave, a smaller one adopts the outline of the mountain, a method that Hokusai often utilizes to give his prints a sense of geometric harmony.

The three boats are *oshiokuri-bune* (押送船, "fast boats"), which were used to transport fish from nearby coastal villages to Edo. In the background, enclosed within a darker shade that accentuates its remoteness, Fuji is framed in a near-perfect semicircle created by a lull in the waves. Although the grandeur of the waves and their swirling movements convey a dramatic intensity, the men in the boat seem confident in the chaos around them; calm and collected, they patiently wait for the wave to pass. The sacred mountain reminds us that everything runs its course, a symbol of peace and tranquility that transcends the turmoil of our world.

Juxtaposing the majesty and stability of Mount Fuji with the fluid churning of the sea, this work emphasizes the dynamic forces of nature by merging Western perspective with Japanese techniques. A master of perspective, Hokusai uses a lowered horizon line and binds it to static and kinetic elements, near and far. The dynamic composition exhibits a tension between human fragility and the powerful forces of nature.

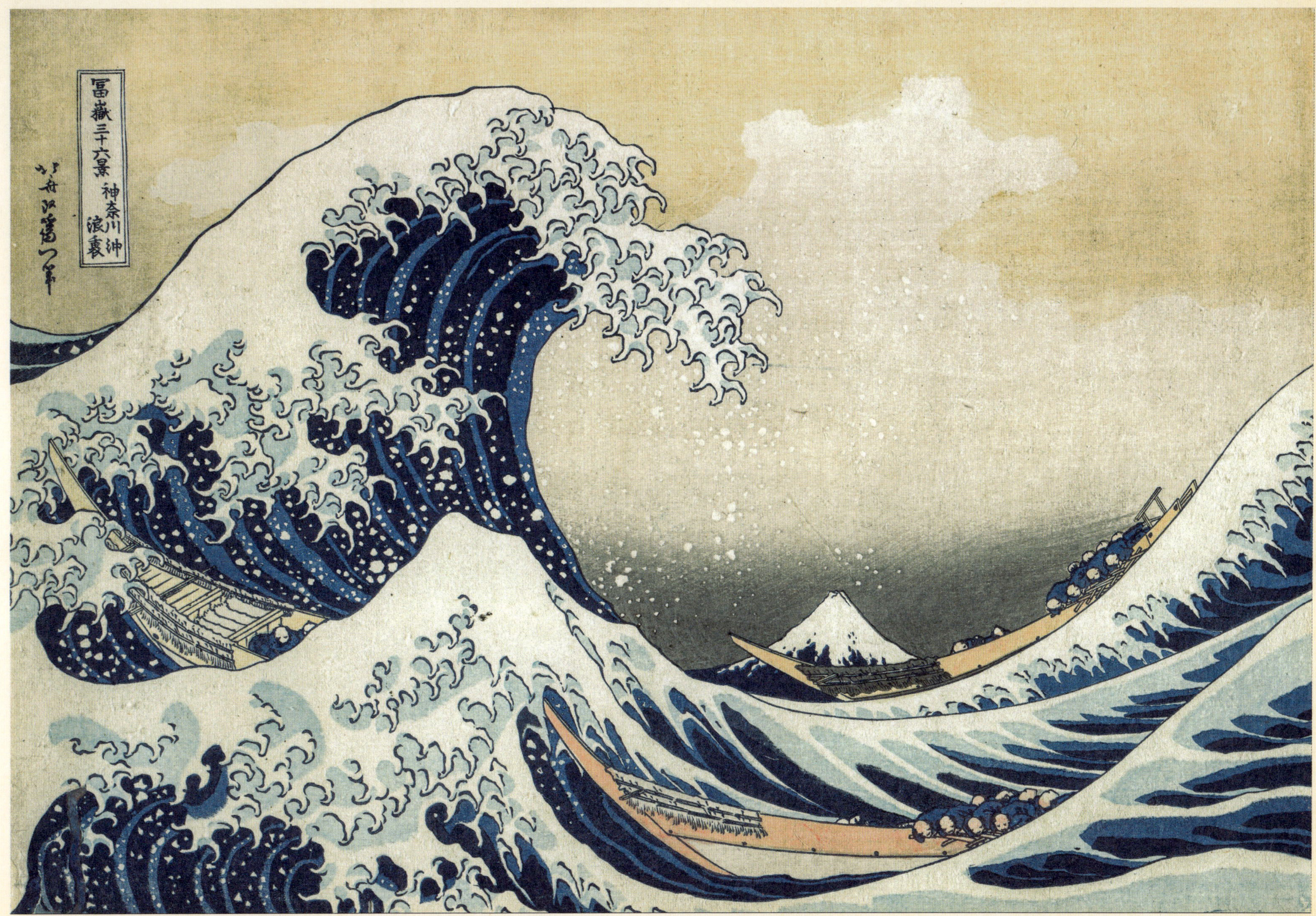

冨嶽三十六景　神奈川沖浪裏
北斎改爲一筆

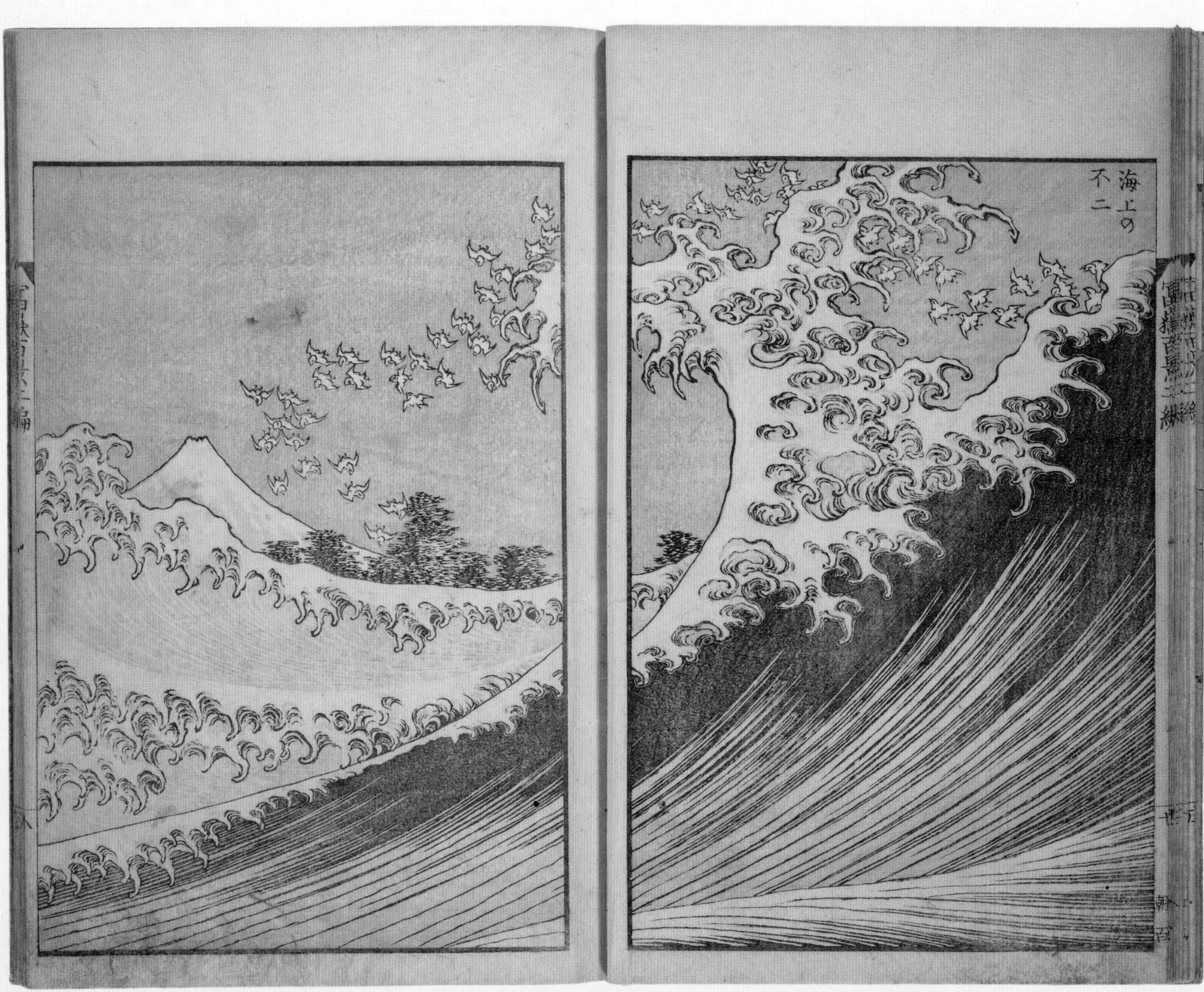

The second volume of Hokusai's subsequent series, *One Hundred Views of Mount Fuji* (*Fugaku hyakkei*), includes an image that mirrors *The Great Wave*—print #40 *Fuji at Sea* (*Kaijo no Fuji*), shown here on the left. However, unlike the original, this print does not include any boats and birds seem to emerge from the foam at the wave's crest.

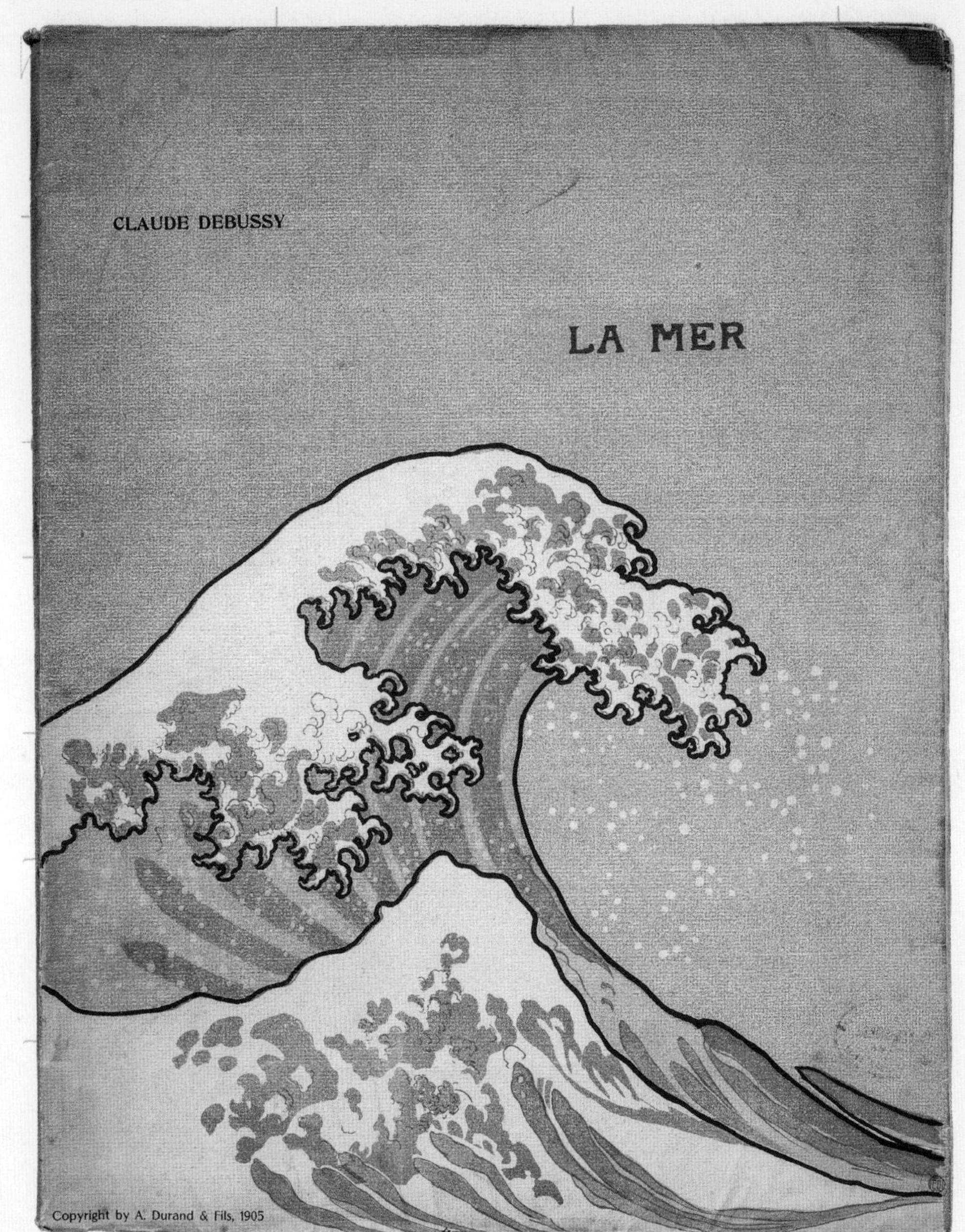

The French composer Claude Debussy (1862–1918), who displayed this print in his studio, composed *La mer* in 1905, and for the first edition of the recording he asked for *The Great Wave* to be featured on the cover.

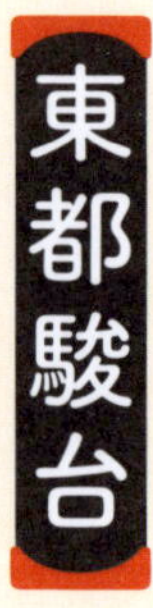

17

Surugadai in Edo

Toto Sundai

This print seems to balance the previous one. Here, too, Fuji can be spotted in the background, while the foreground hones in on mundane human activities. Sundai, known today as Surugadai and located in Tokyo's Kanda district, housed the *shogun*'s servants during the Edo period. Thanks to its elevation, this was a popular spot from which to view the city and the mountain. The print is dominated by a sloped hill on the left and a large protruding roof at the bottom right that partially obstructs the view of Fuji.

On the street, people of different social classes, workers and travelers scatter in many directions. On the lower left, a samurai is accompanied by three servants who carry his luggage; next to them, a street vendor uses a fan to shield himself from the sun. All around them other people can be seen walking up and down the hill, including a hat-wearing pilgrim on the left.

Hokusai uses small dots and shading for the ground. These techniques, together with the short lines and pronounced curves with which he drew the trees, were adopted from Chinese painting, an art form he studied throughout his life.

As in *The Great Wave* (#16), Fuji is framed here by a semi-circle formed by the roof and the yellow contours of the hill. The different elevations, the diversity of colors and the combination of buildings and natural elements make this work extremely dynamic. The composition is reminiscent of print #21 *Lower Meguro* (*Shimo Meguro*).

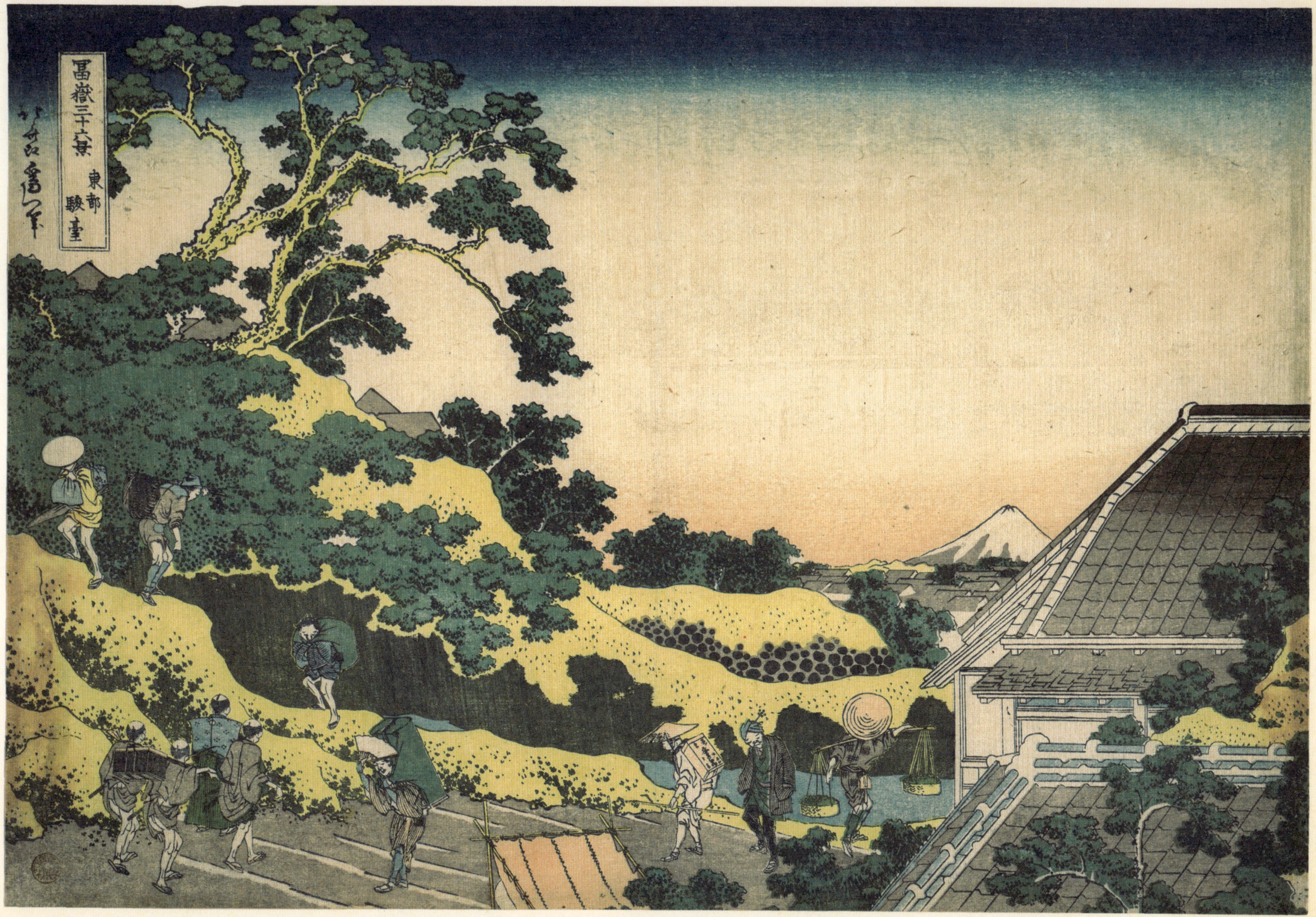
冨嶽三十六景
東都
駿臺

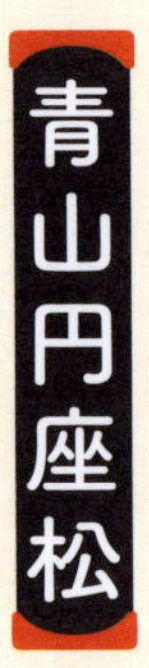

18

Cushion Pine at Aoyama

Aoyama Enza No Matsu

Once again, Fuji sits serenely in the backdrop behind a combination of human, natural and architectural elements. The mountain, emerging imposingly from a low mist, adopts a similar shape to the cluster of famed pine trees below from which the print derives its name. These reside in the garden of Ryuganji, a Zen temple in Harajuku (Tokyo) and a popular observation spot for admiring Fuji.

The pine tree was famous for the expansive breadth of its roots, which forced other smaller pines to be planted around it in a circle. Given that Hokusai could not have seen the mountain with such large dimensions from this location, the print is a good example of how the artist combined reality and imagination to achieve his desired effect.

At the front right, a group of travelers have stopped for a break to enjoy the view over a drink; meanwhile, a man points toward the mountain rising above the mist, urging a young boy to look in its direction. On the left, another man is concealed behind the pines, only his legs visible, as he rakes fallen needles from the trees.

White streaks of low-lying clouds allow Fuji to stand out against the sky with dramatic effect.

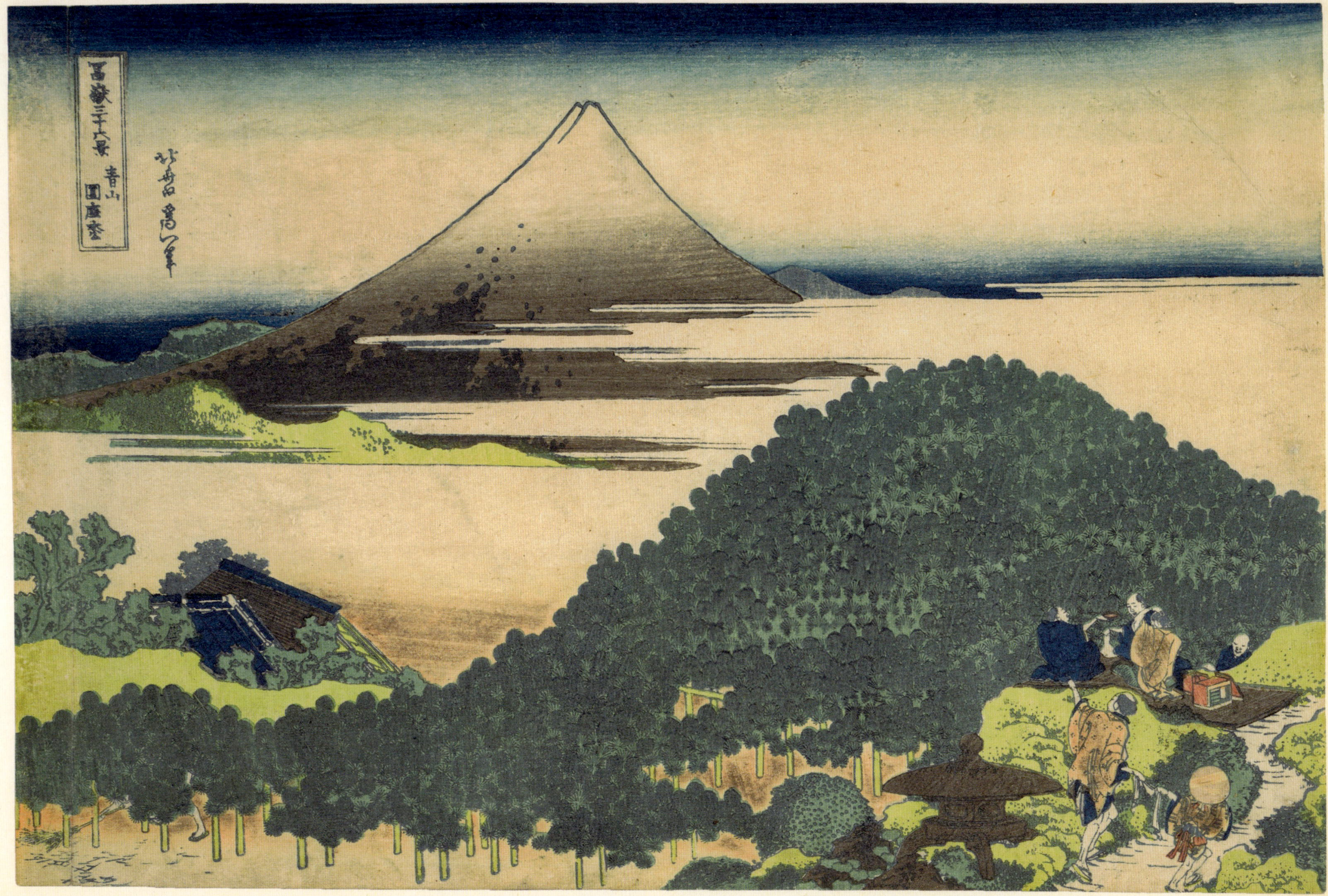

冨嶽三十六景 青山圓座松
前北斎卍筆

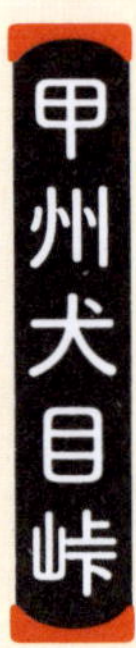

19

The Inume Pass in Kai Province

Koshu Inume Toge

Fuji again rises majestically above a group of men going about their daily affairs. It is sunset; the top of the mountain is covered in just a little snow and the color of the vegetation announces the start of summer. The men are probably on their way home: at the bottom, two of them are followed by loaded horses, with two more at the top. The leader is facing toward Fuji. The huge clouds and the grandeur of Fuji are amplified by the tiny scale of the men and their horses, underscoring the distance between them and the mountain.The warm tones and the hunched backs of the four wayfarers and their animals juxtaposes a sense of fatigue from their labors amidst great scenic beauty.

The province of Kai corresponds to today's Yamanashi Prefecture west of Tokyo, a landlocked mountainous region.

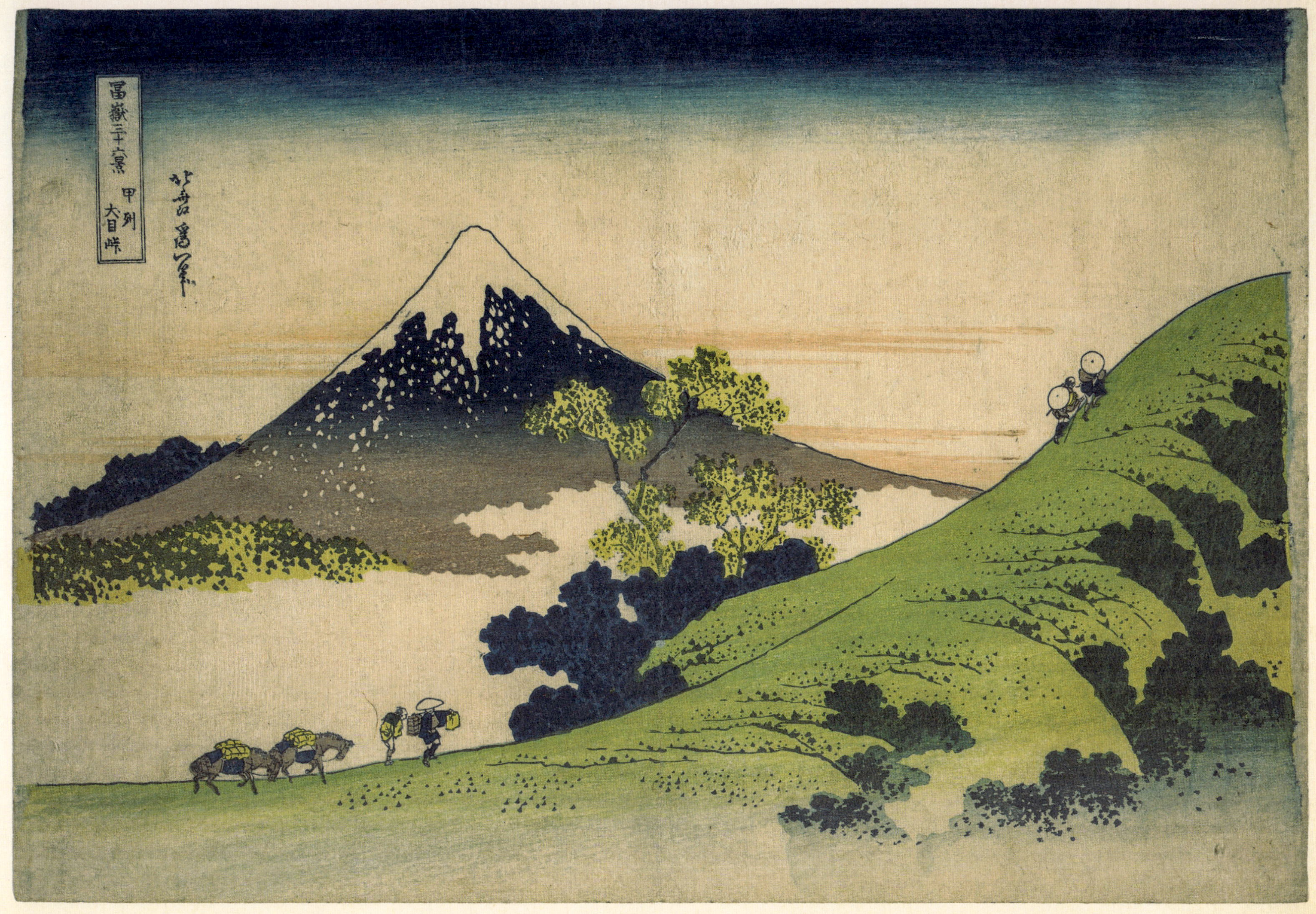

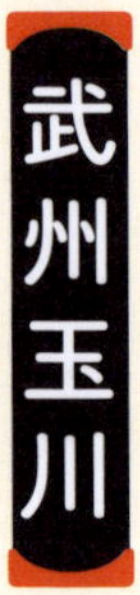

20

Tama River in Musashi Province

Bushu Tamagawa

This print is characterized by a stark, almost geometric composition that divides it into bands. Let's start from the bottom. First is the land, depicted in shades of green and brown; a man traverses it together with his horse laden with bundles of branches. Next is the sea, which fades from white into blue; three men ferry wood across the water in a boat, its bow and oar guiding our eyes toward Fuji. Beyond, a bank of dense fog abruptly cuts off the sea and creates a separate, ethereal space—a seemingly sacred realm that graces us with the view of Fuji. The last band, despite occupying only the upper quarter of the frame, dominates the entire image with its presence.

Compared to the previous few prints, Hokusai limits his use of colors here, preferring cold blue tones. The blue of the water is repeated in the trees of the foreground. These tones, together with the placid water and man leading his horse on bank, provide a sense of peace.

The Tama River, which flows west of Tokyo, is one of Japan's most important waterways.

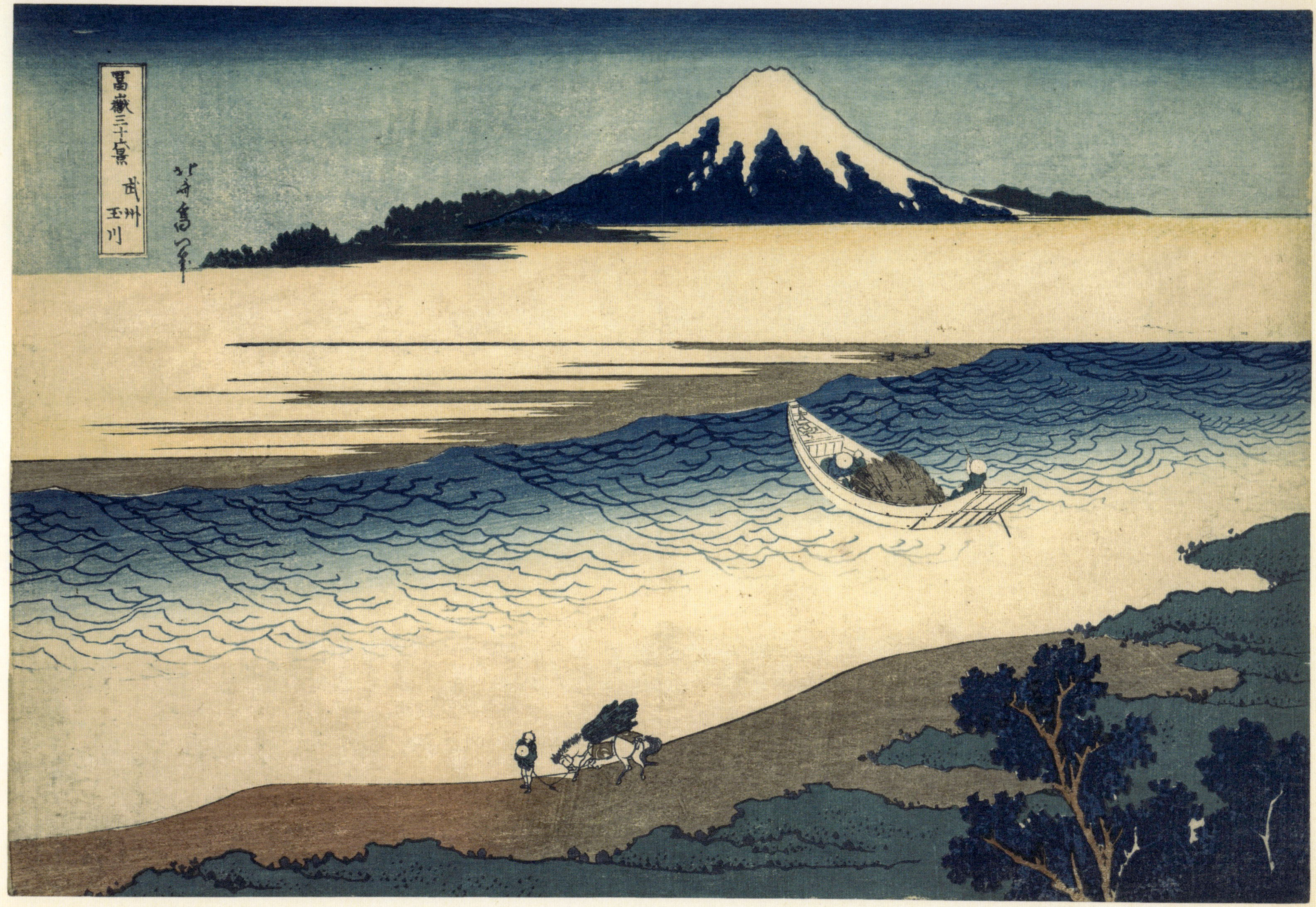

冨嶽三十六景
武州
玉川
北斎画筆

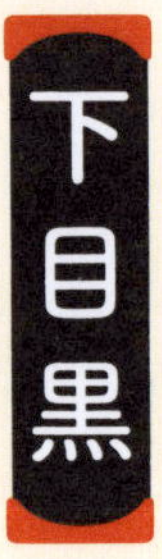

21

Lower Meguro

Shimo Meguro

Hokusai here chooses Meguro, a place among the hills in Edo—then famous for hawk hunting—for a pastoral scene among cultivated fields and huts, where men and women are busy with their daily chores. No one seems to be paying attention to Fuji. To the right, two falcon handlers can be seen arguing as a man kneels in front of them, probably having asked him for information. The man is looking at them but is perhaps also catching a glimpse of the distant mountain. Further to the left, a woman tends to her child; further on, a farmer lugs a hoe on his shoulders. The latter appears out of proportion with the rest of the figures, but his presence creates an equilibrium with the tall pines that rise up from the landscape on the right. Together, they create a frame for Fuji, almost hidden behind the hills and vegetation. The terrain consists of terraced fields that gradually rise on the right, while on the left this upward movement is mirrored by the tall roofs of the dwellings. Thatched roofs were typically used for farmers' houses. The volcano blends into the landscape in such a way that it is barely noticeable at first glance.

Meguro is today a busy district of Tokyo, but in Hokusai's time it was a small village outside the city.

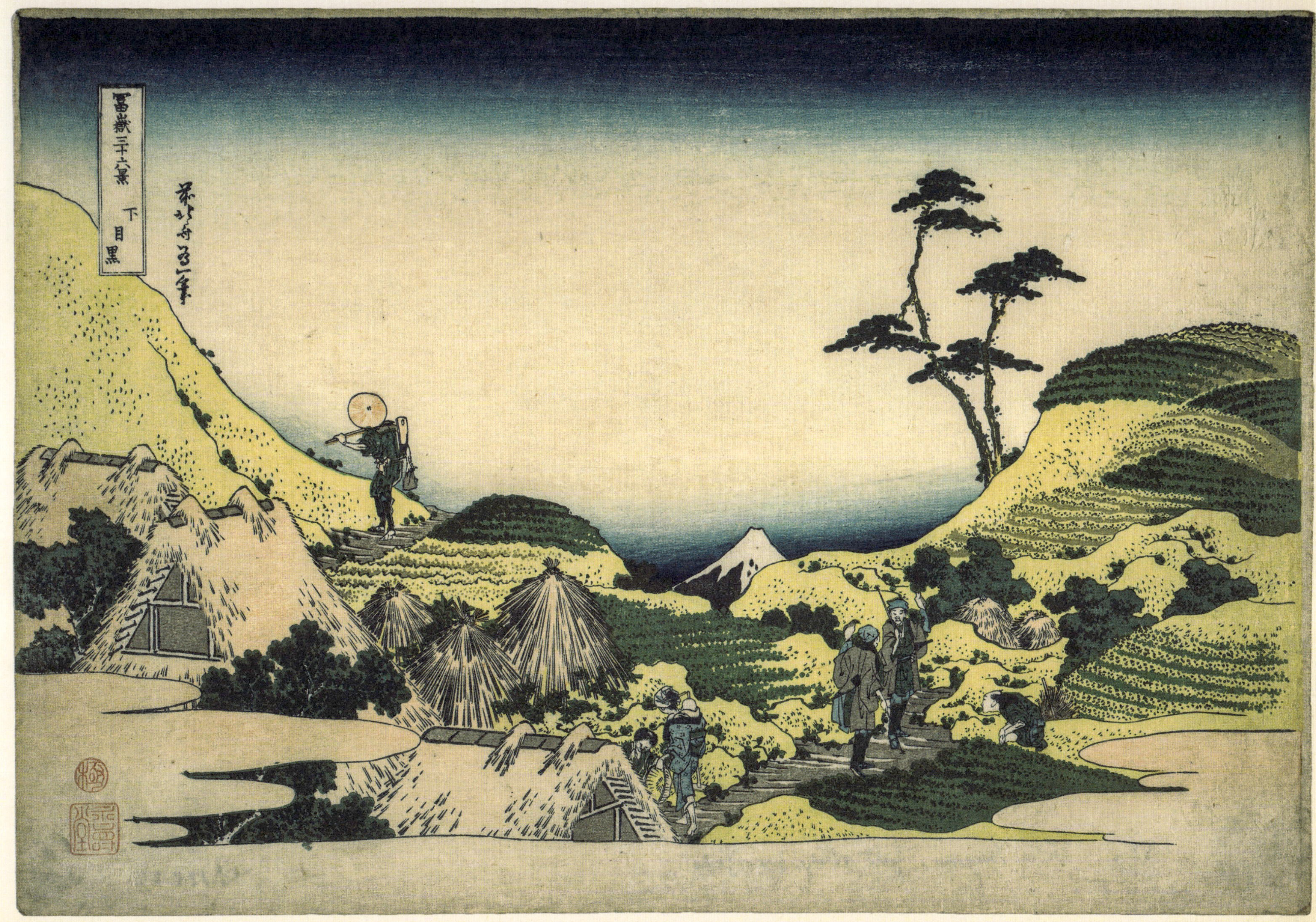
冨嶽三十六景
下目黒

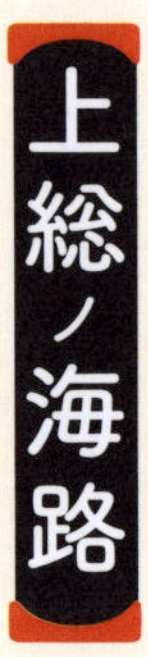

22

At Sea Off Kazusa

Kazusa No Kairo

Two large cargo-filled ships set sail with the wind at their backs. The sailors are below deck, visible through a small window. These seafaring vessels, different from the boats that maneuver the rivers, are here preparing to cross the ocean from Kazusa province. Hokusai presents them in extraordinary detail.

During the Edo period, there were no passenger ships on the main sea routes. Pleasure boats and ferries exclusively transported passengers on rivers and canals. Maritime cargo ships could, however, accommodate passengers in a large cabin beneath the upper deck. They were built with fir or cedar and designed for both sailing and rowing.

Fuji is framed in the distance by a large triangle formed by ropes that hold the boat's sail. The triangular shapes created by the ropes and sails mimic the mountain's silhouette.

The horizon is curved; at the time, the theory that the earth is spherical had become common knowledge among the Japanese through trade contact with the Dutch.

The intense blue of the water finds a visual parallel in a blue band that spans the horizon and an even darker hue at the top of the sky, creating a sense of depth.

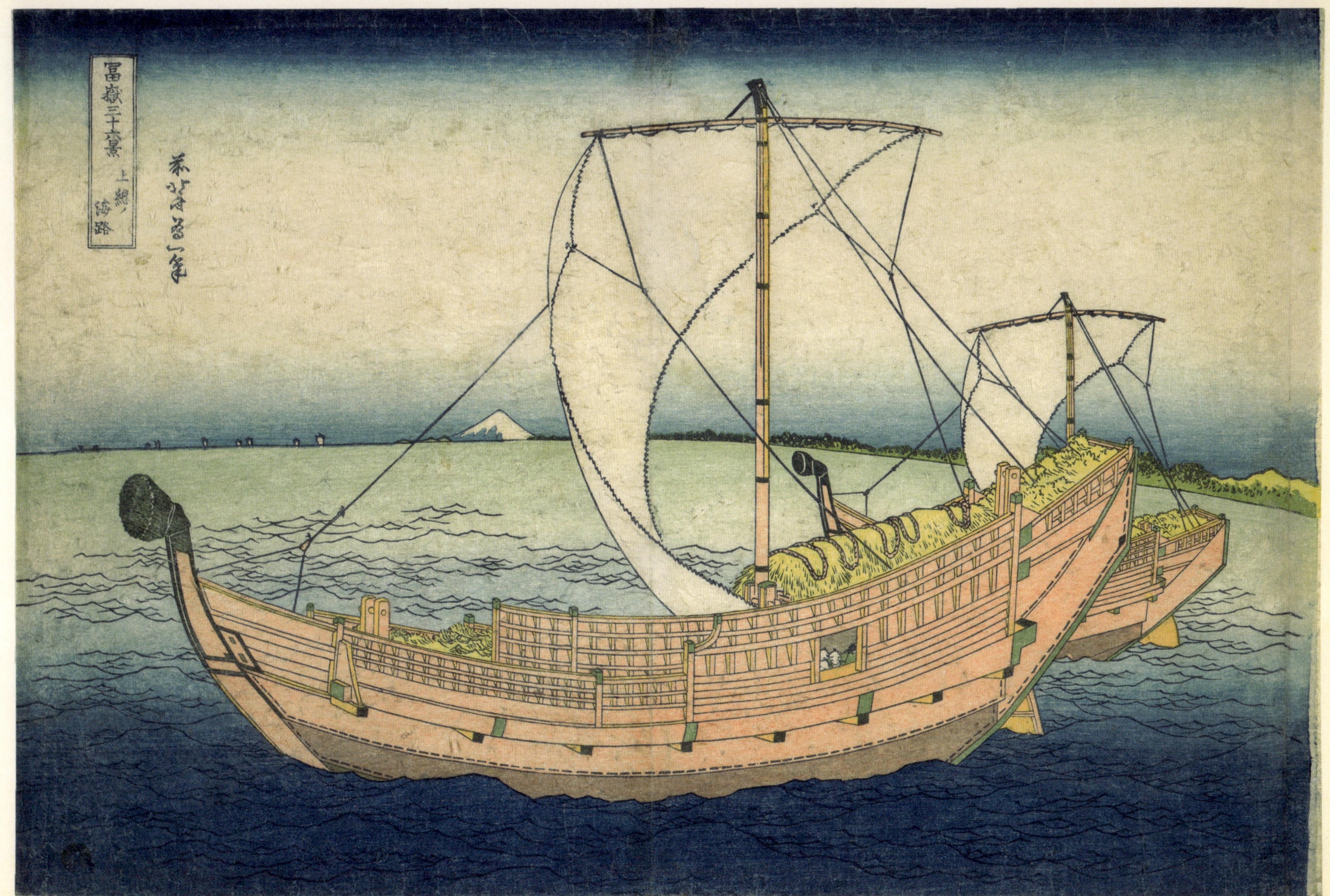
冨嶽三十六景 上總ノ海路
前北齋為一筆

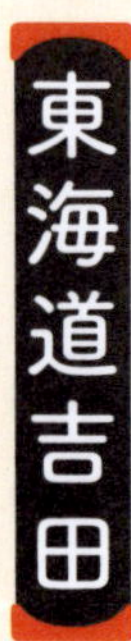

23

Yoshida on the Tokaido

Tokaido Yoshida

A group of travelers are enjoying the view of Fuji from Yoshida Post Stop, number 34 on the Tokaido. A maid points out the volcano to the two female travelers on the balustrade. Around them, the porters are resting, one is adjusting his straw sandals by beating them with a hammer, and another is wiping sweat from his forehead while smoking a pipe.

Hokusai's focus here is less on Fuji itself and more about human interactions with the mountain. The figures are spread out in a loosely-triangular manner that hints at the shape of Fuji. The structure of the terrace frames the image like a painting within a painting. On the lantern at the top we can read, from right to left, the name of the inn: 不二見茶屋 *Fujimi Chaya* ("Tea House with a View of Fuji"). The characters used for Fuji are not the usual ones, 富士, but the homophones 不二, meaning "peerless." On the panels to the right, one can read from above 御茶津希 (*ochatsuke*, rice with spilled green tea) and 根元吉田ほくち (*nemoto Yoshida hokuchi*, the district's specialty). On the round hats near the doorframe, Hokusai printed the trademark of his publisher, Eijudo.

Although it is the only print in the series to show the interior of a building, the composition is reminiscent of that in print #33 *Sazai Hall at the Temple of the Five Hundred Arhats* (*Gohyaku Rakanji Sazaido*), where travelers look at the mountain from an outdoor terrace. This print, however, is more dynamic.

Hokusai had already made many prints and paintings depicting not only female beauties, but also women and men of all classes. This work displayed his masterful ability to transpose those techniques and aesthetics onto a series of landscapes as well.

Yoshida, now part of the present town of Toyohashi, was a famous castle town on the Tokaido road.

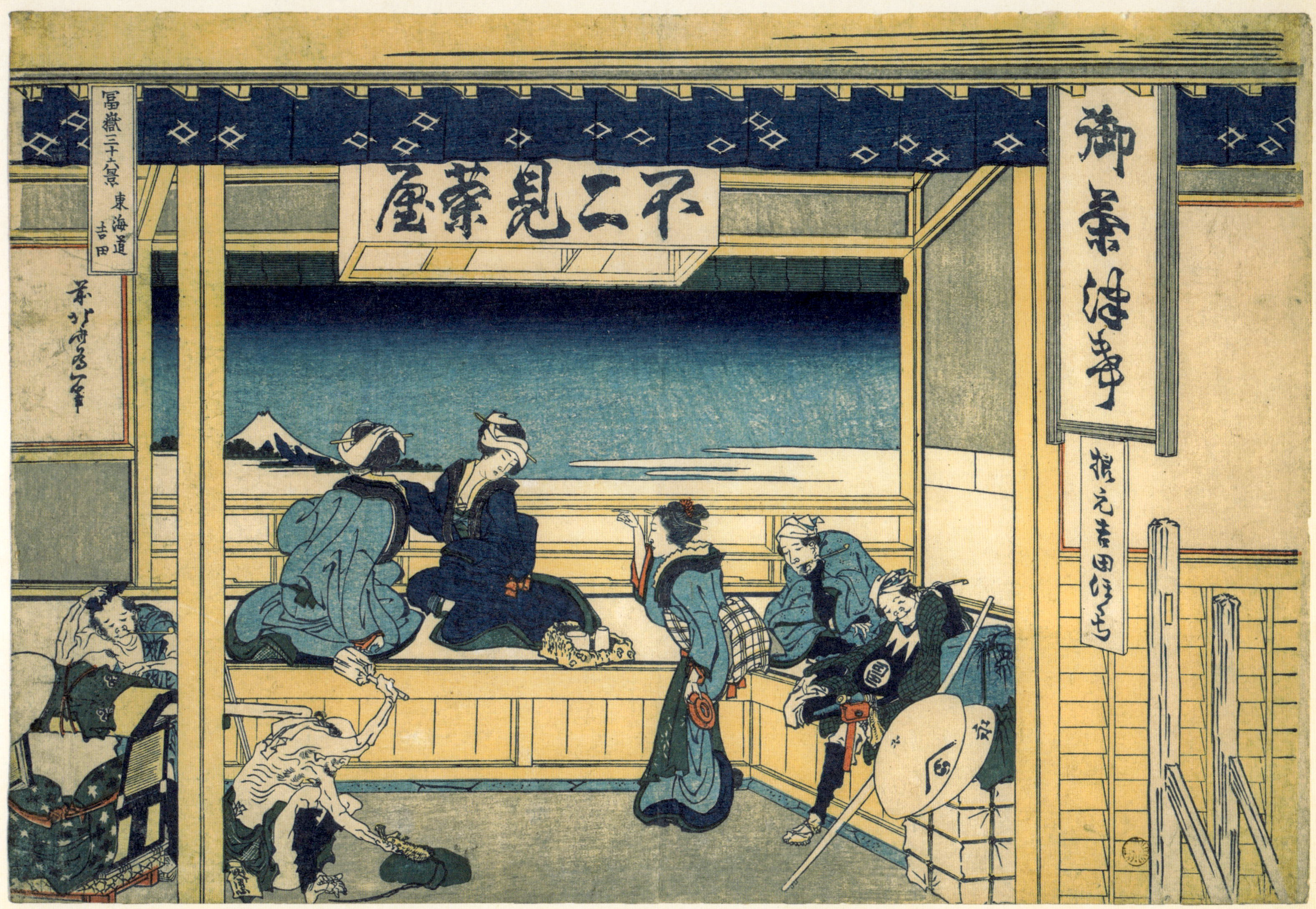
冨嶽三十六景 東海道 吉田
不二見茶屋
前北斎為一筆
御茶漬
御休処
揚元吉田住

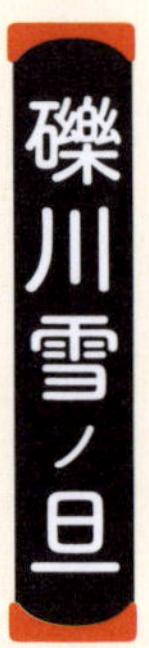

24

Morning After the Snow at Koishikawa

Koishikawa Yuki No Ashita

It is a winter morning. Fuji, and the entire landscape around it, are covered by an overnight blanket of snow. From the second floor of a teahouse, a group of travelers—men and women—enjoy the view. One woman points to the mountain while an attendant brings a tray filled with plates of food.

The people in this scene, framed within the terrace, appear like a picture within a picture (as in print #23). Color and animated activity are concentrated in this tiny space while everything else conforms to the stillness and silence of the snow. If it were not for that finger pointing into the distance, the two would remain separate; instead, they interact, inviting us to shift our gaze from the group to the mountain. The woman also points to three small birds flying in the white sky, the only other hint of movement in the image.

Hokusai excelled in presenting water in all its forms from placid to rushing, but rarely depicted snowy landscapes. Perhaps he was disinclined to deal with snow because it covered the details he liked to render so carefully. This print is therefore a rare example of a snowy scene in his portfolio. The landscape is further softened by blue rather than black outlines, a feature common to all thirty-six original prints in the series.

Now located in the modern Bunkyo district of Tokyo, the Koishikawa farming area was famous for its view of Mount Fuji. The area's many inns also made it a popular place for visitors.

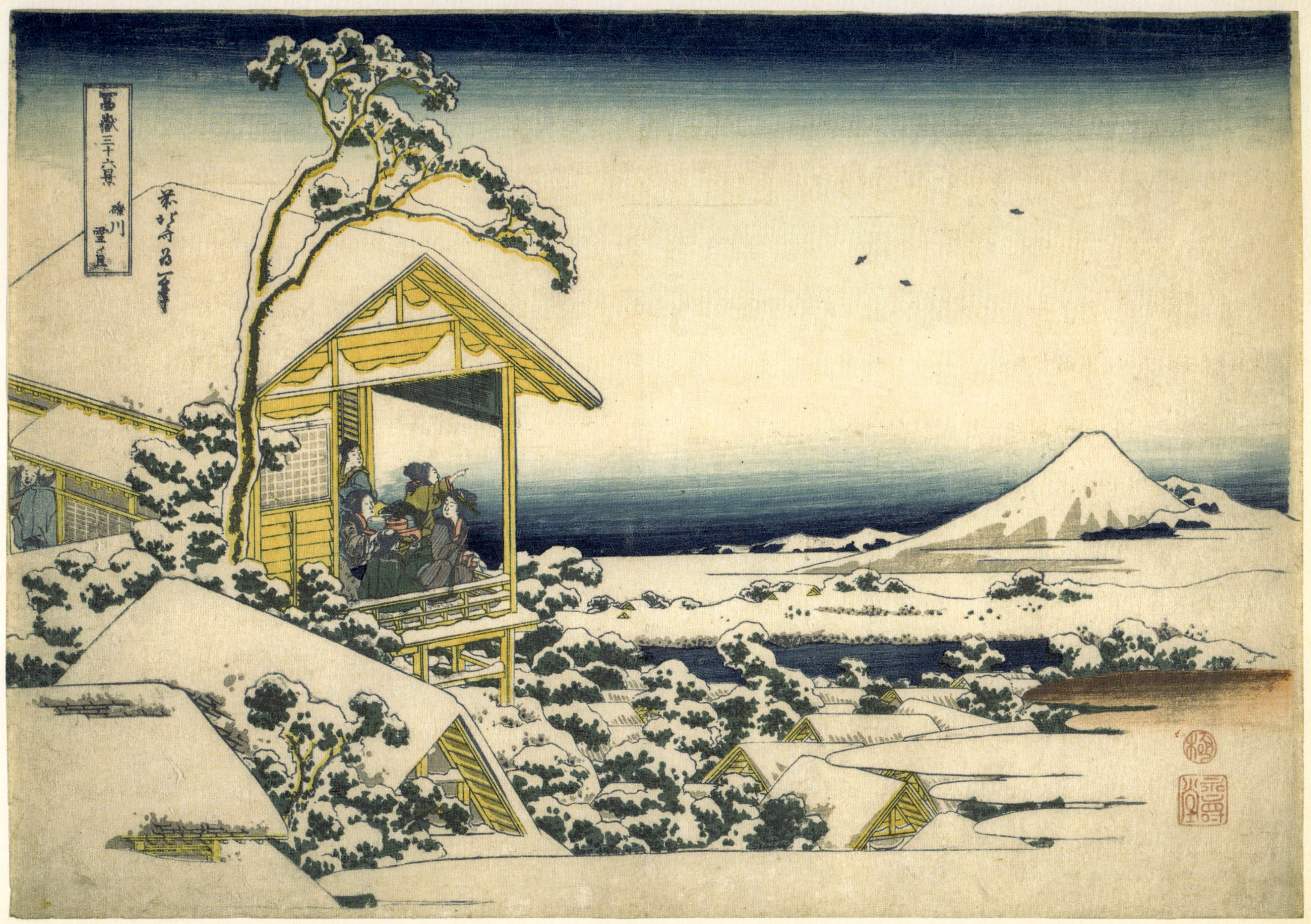

冨嶽三十六景　礫川雪ノ旦
前北斎為一筆

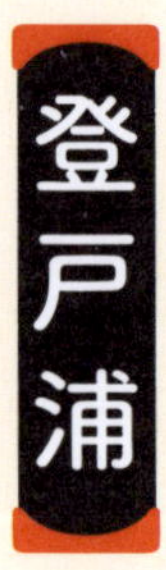

25

Noboto Bay

Noboto No Ura

On a warm summer day, men and women collect shells on the beach of Noboto village during low tide; above them, two *torii* gates mark the entrance to a *shinto* shrine. Two men have already filled their baskets with shellfish as another is just arriving. Further to the left, a man and woman argue while holding their empty baskets, perhaps over where to best look; two other pickers, already in the water, are busy at work. On the left, two children can be seen horsing around.

That the larger *torii* frames Fuji emphasizes its sacredness. As usual, Hokusai places the mountain within a geometric structure.

Noboto, a small fishing village, was located on the east coast of Edo Bay. Its shallow waters, spread over a large area, were ideal for collecting shellfish. On the hill above the beach sat the small Towatari shrine to which the two *torii* belonged. Since 1990, the shrine has been moved to today's Chiba Prefecture, southeast of Tokyo, where it sits on dry land.

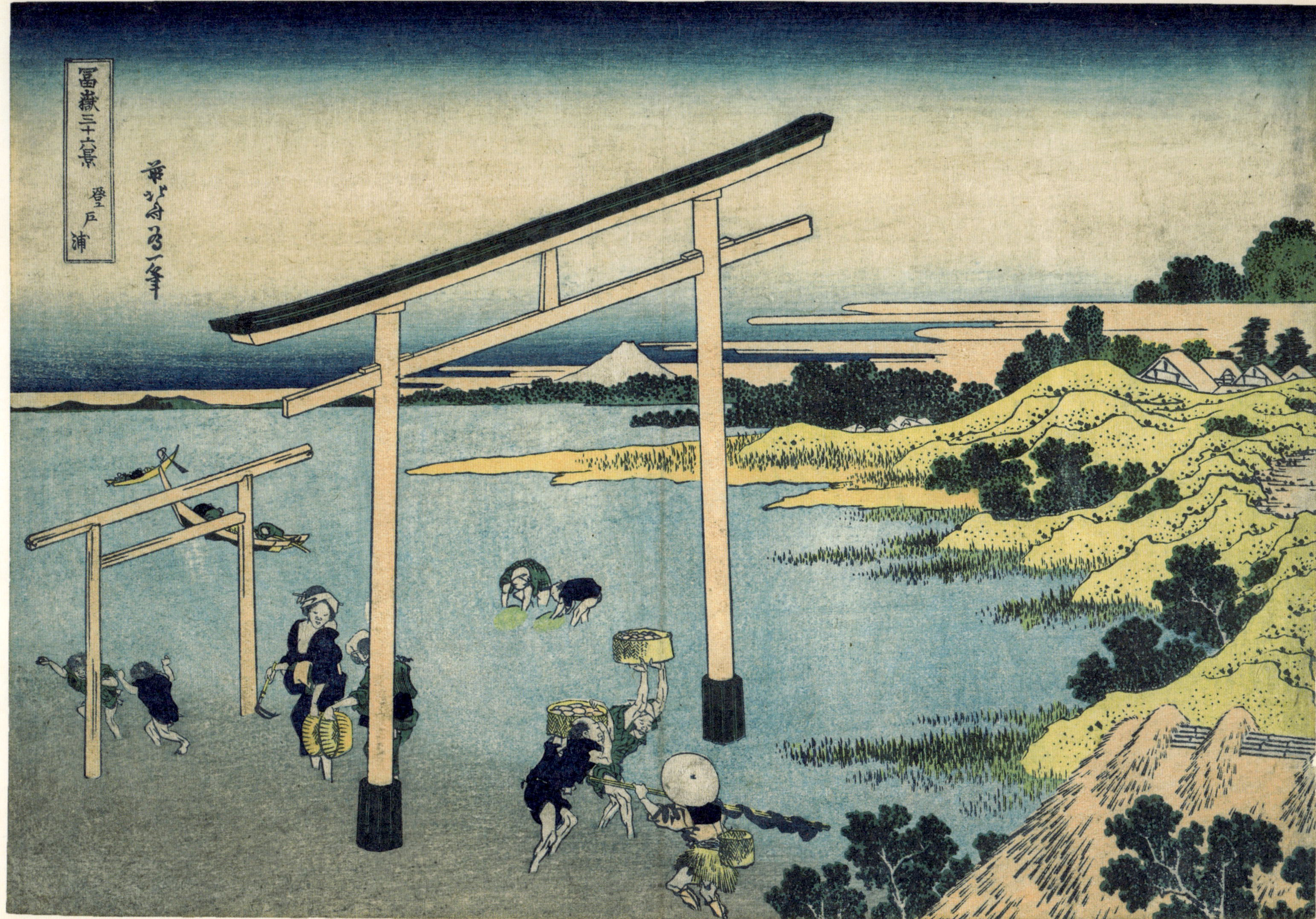

冨嶽三十六景　登戸浦
北斎改爲一筆

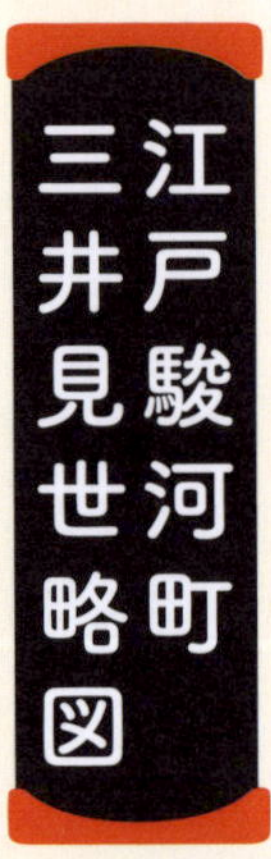

Mitsui Shop at Surugacho in Edo

Edo Surugacho Mitsui Mise Ryakuzu

Two shop houses frame Fuji in the center of the picture. On the right, three men are repairing the roof of the famous Mitsui kimono shop, owned by the Echigoya family, which stood on what was then Edo's busiest street: Surugacho, north of Nihonbashi (print #32). The volcano is observed from a high vantage point above the street and between the two buildings, and is drawn with an exaggerated perspective. The signs at the bottom left and right advertise the shops' products (clothing, ropes and braided threads) and indicate the accepted method of payment (reduced prices for cash).

The Mitsui shop was very successful precisely because it adopted a new business practice where payment was made in cash at the time of sale, instead of debiting accounts which were then settled by customers once or twice a year. In doing so, the shop could sell at reduced prices. The shop was the progenitor of the well-known chain of Mitsukoshi department stores that still exists today!

The roofs' triangular profiles emulate the shape of the mountain, giving rhythm to the image. The way in which the men are depicted, as if dancing, exudes a dynamism that simultaneously fills the image with grace. Two kites soar above the shop. The Japanese liked to fly kites on the first days of the year, suggesting that New Year's had just passed. The kite on the left reads 壽 (*kotobuki / ju*), which means longevity, but is also one of the characters that make up the name of the series' publisher, Nishimuraya Yohachi's publishing house Eijudo (永壽堂)—the omen of the New Year thus doubles as an advertisement.

Suruga was the old name of the region where Mount Fuji was located. From Surugacho, the street that gave the print its name, it was possible to see Fuji during Hokusai's time. However, the view is now obstructed by tall buildings.

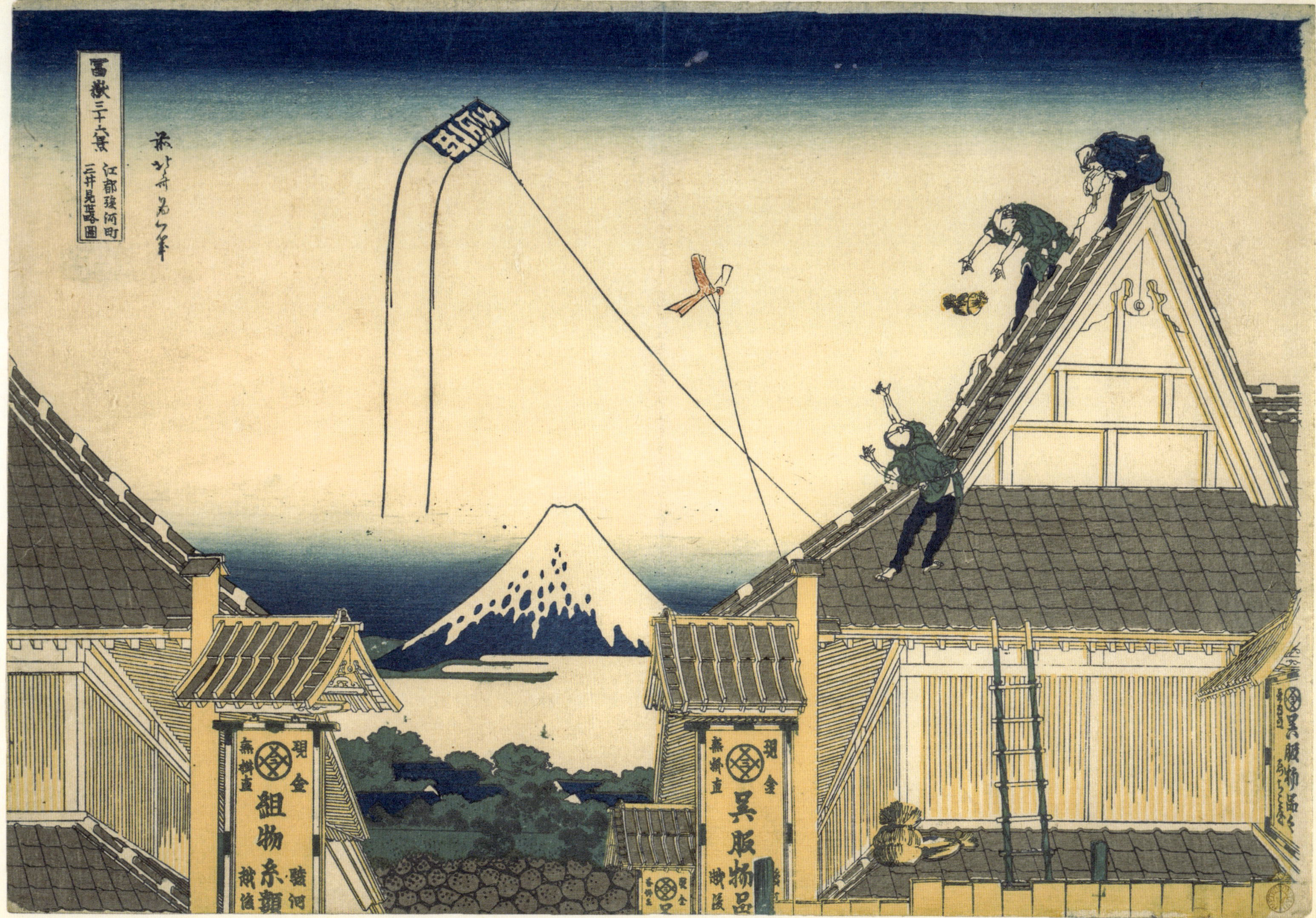
冨嶽三十六景
江都駿河町
三井見世略圖
前北齋為一筆
現金
無掛直
組物糸類
駿河
現金
無掛直
吳服物品
越後
吳服物品

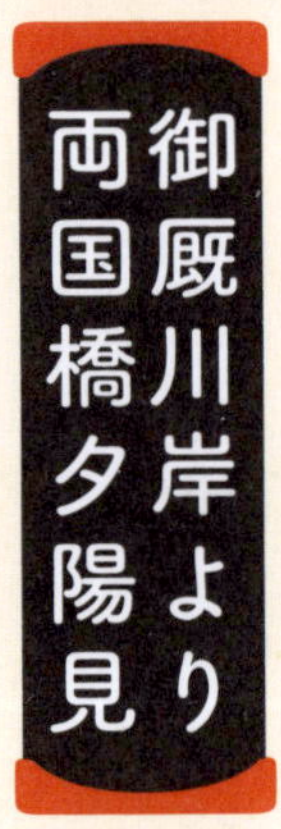

Viewing the Sunset Over Ryogoku Bridge from the Onmaya Embankment

Onmayagashi Yori Ryogokubashi Sekiyo O Miru

A ferry loaded with passengers sets off across the Sumida River. The ferryman and the passengers seem to express the diversity of Edo's population: vendors, samurai, travelers, men, women, monks. On the bow, a man in a moss-green kimono sits alone, almost curled into himself. The clothing suggests that he has made a long and arduous journey. A samurai, wearing a brown *haori* from which two katana handles protrude, leans against the boat's side, lifting his headgear in contemplation of Mount Fuji. Next to him, a man wearing a blue summer *yukata* decorated with large blue stars rinses a rag.

Behind him a bald man leans forward on his cane. Standing in the middle of the group is a merchant in an indigo kimono with a green *furoshiki* down his back. Next to him is a woman wearing a traditional white bandana; on the other side is a bird catcher, distinguished by his tall staff, who dons a striped kimono, a green *haori* and a straw hat. In front of him, two men converse with each other. Another woman sits at the stern, holding open a large umbrella. The ferryman, having folded up his sleeves and his *kasuri* garment, reveals his traditional loincloth underneath (*fundoshi*). Another woman in a nearby boat washes her

cloth in the river. Most of the crowd seem indifferent to the beauty of dark blue Fuji in the distance; the only exceptions are the ferryman, who is likely most accustomed to the view, and, perhaps, the merchant standing in the center.

The curve of the boat inverts the arch of the Ryogoku Bridge; Fuji rises on its right-most extreme. It captures the moment when sunset slips into evening and the waters become peacefully calm, as if to presage the stillness of the day's end. Despite the tranquility of the scene, emboldened by the soft waves and twilight hues, the composition is dynamic, alternating between straight and curved lines and presenting a varied assortment of human characters.

While the foreground is clearly delineated with blue lines, the view in the background, with the bridge, the boats and the distant shore, gradually fades into amorphous shapes and undifferentiated tones.

This ferry port was famous for its view of Fuji. In Hokusai's time, people gathered around Ryogoku Bridge to admire the summer fireworks, a tradition that continues to this day. In the Edo period, a network of large rivers and canals provided cheap public transport for everyone.

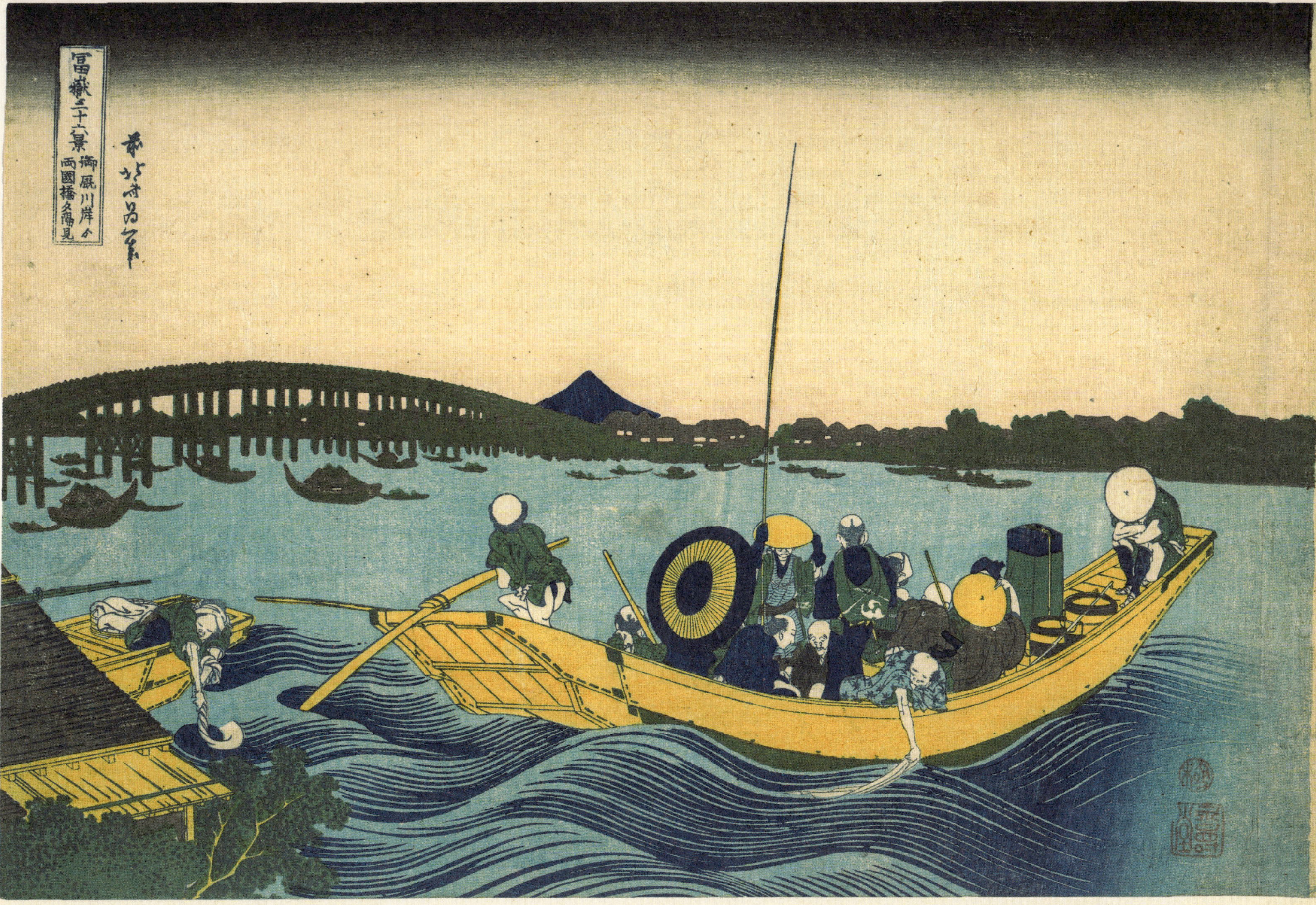
冨嶽三十六景
御厩川岸ゟ両國橋夕陽見
前北斎卍筆

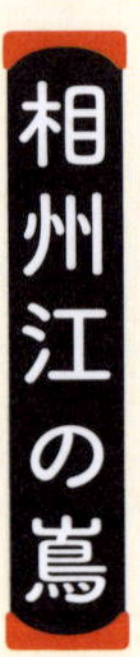

28

Enoshima in Sagami Province

Soshu Enoshima

Enoshima, a small island off Kamakura southwest of Tokyo, was famous for its shrine to Benzaiten and was an important pilgrimage destination during the Edo period.

Benzaiten was one of the seven goddesses of good fortune, the embodiment of music and entertainment, and also the herald of good luck, longevity and victory in war. The entire island is dedicated to her as the deity who, according to legend, rose up from the depths of the sea in the 6th century.

The viewpoint is from an elevated position on the mainland. Above a blanket of low-lying fog in the foreground, pilgrims can be seen making their way toward the island, including one on horseback. On the island, one can see a few shops and inns as well as the temple's pagoda. Two large stone lanterns stand guard at the village's front steps.

Fuji is far away on the right, separated from the temple and its pilgrims, surrounded by water, clouds and land. The mountain is partly obstructed by a small boat whose raised mast and sail mimic the shape of the volcano. Hokusai uses cloudy dots to depict foam in the water, suggesting that it is low tide. The vegetation of the island uses the same style, reminiscent of both the Western technique of pointillism and traditional Chinese painting.

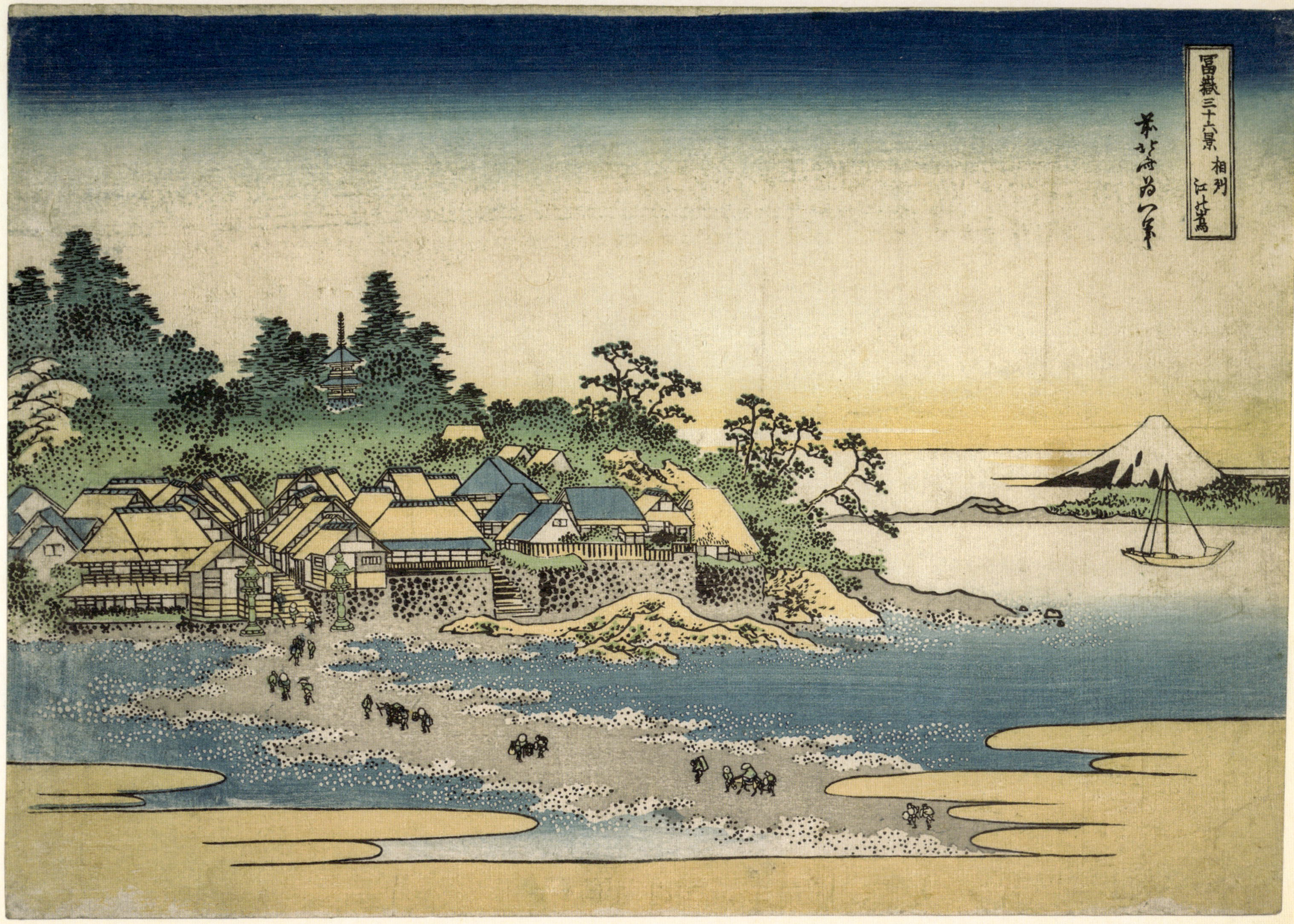
冨嶽三十六景　相刕　江之嶋
前北斎為一筆

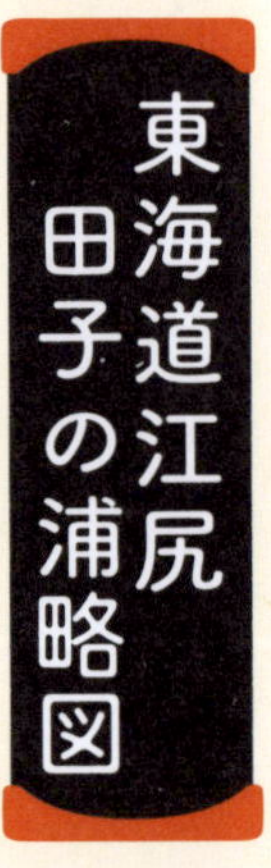

29

Tago Bay Near Ejiri
on the Tokaido

Tokaido Ejiri Tago No Ura Ryakuzu

In the foreground, two fishing boats navigate the waves of a choppy sea, its rocky currents personified by the fatigue of the rowers. The man on the bow of the first boat casts his net into the sea. Like his counterpart on the second boat, he steadies himself against the undulating currents. The curvature of the boats echo the shape of Fuji. On the shore, an intense salt harvesting operation is underway. The commotion of the waves and boats stand in stark contrast to the uniformly colored rows of fog that partially conceal the mountain.

Tago Bay has long been recognized as a place to enjoy views of Fuji. It is featured in poems as far back as the *Man'yoshu*, the first known collection of Japanese poetry written around the middle of the 8th century.

Ejiri, the 18th station on the Tokaido road, is in today's Shizuoka Prefecture southwest of Tokyo. It is also depicted in print #8.

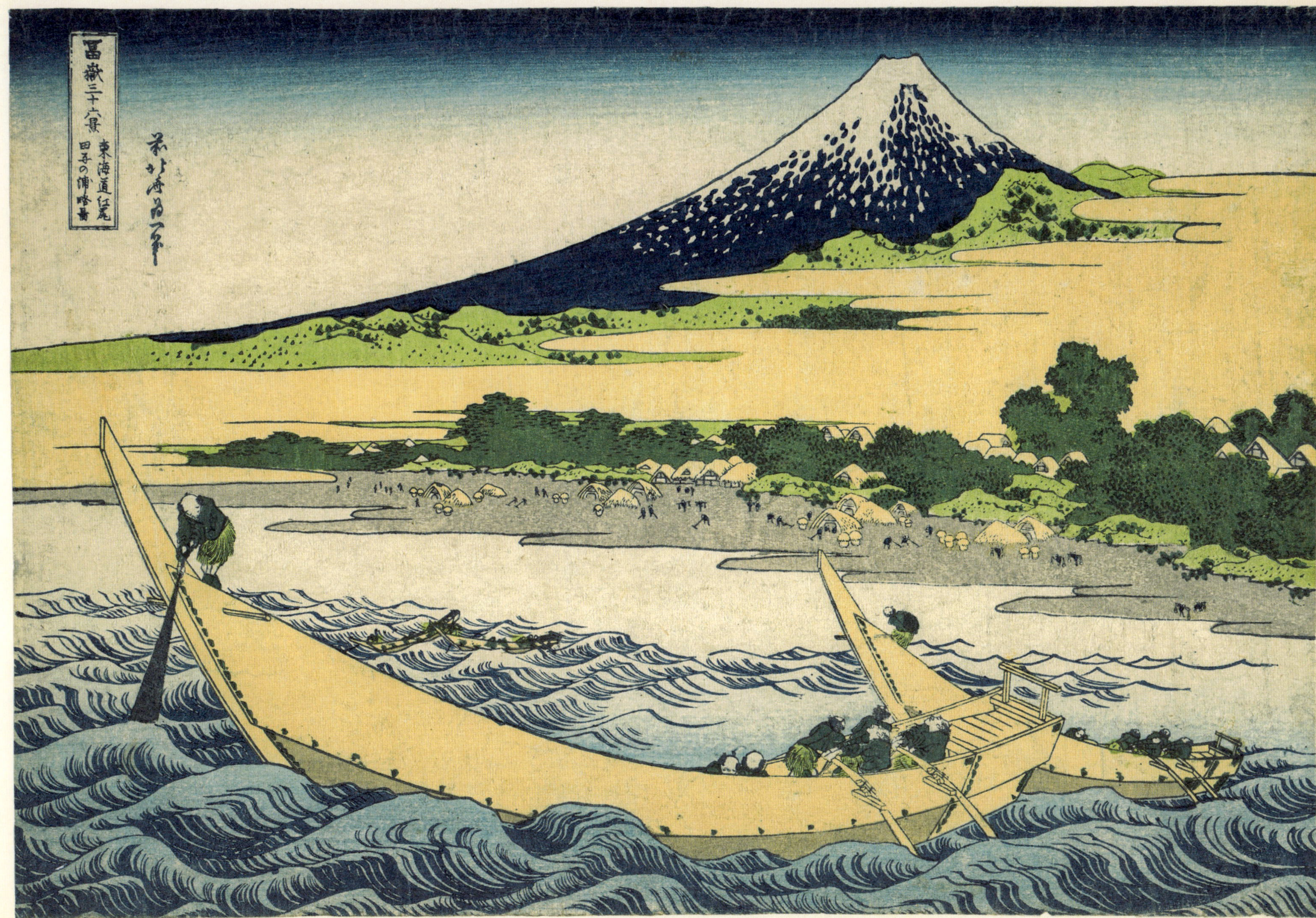

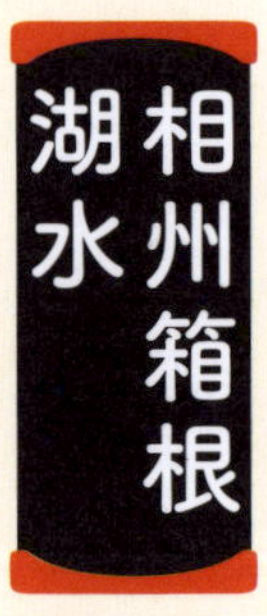

30

The Lake at Hakone in Sagami Province

Soshu Hakone Kosui

The mountainous region near Hakone southeast of Fuji was the most impassable area for Tokaido travelers. Across approximately 19 miles (30 kilometers) between the Odawara and Mishima stations, the road climbed and descended, skirting Lake Ashinoko at high altitude.

However, all of this is absent in Hokusai's print, which softens the landscape with rounded shapes and bright colors. Using clouds and mists rendered in the traditional stylized form called *suyari gasumi* typical of *yamato-e* painting (a traditional Japanese style from the Heian period), the artist succeeds in creating the illusion of depth even though the print is flat. The viewer's attention is thus drawn toward the sacred mountain. The round hills and bright tones are further reminiscent of traditional *yamato-e*.

Between the clouds and hills is a dense forest where, on the right, one can glimpse the buildings of the Hakone shrine. Lake Ashinoko shows no ripples on its surface. This is one of the few prints in the series devoid of human or animal figures.

Sagami Province, located in today's Kanagawa Prefecture between Tokyo and Fuji, was famous for its views of the mountain behind Ashinoko, here partially shrouded in mist. Hakone was one of the Tokaido's most important stations and is now a well-known spa resort located to the west of the capital.

In 1618, early in the Edo period, a checkpoint was set up there to inspect travelers, particularly women. This was to enforce the *sankin kotai*, the policy of "alternate attendance" where the shogunate required *daimyo* (feudal lords) to alternate each year between living in the capital and their home domain, while their wives and daughters were kept permanently in Tokyo. Many women felt constrained by what felt like imprisonment and so tried to escape. To prevent this, the shogunate set up these checkpoints to verify the identity and permits of travelers.

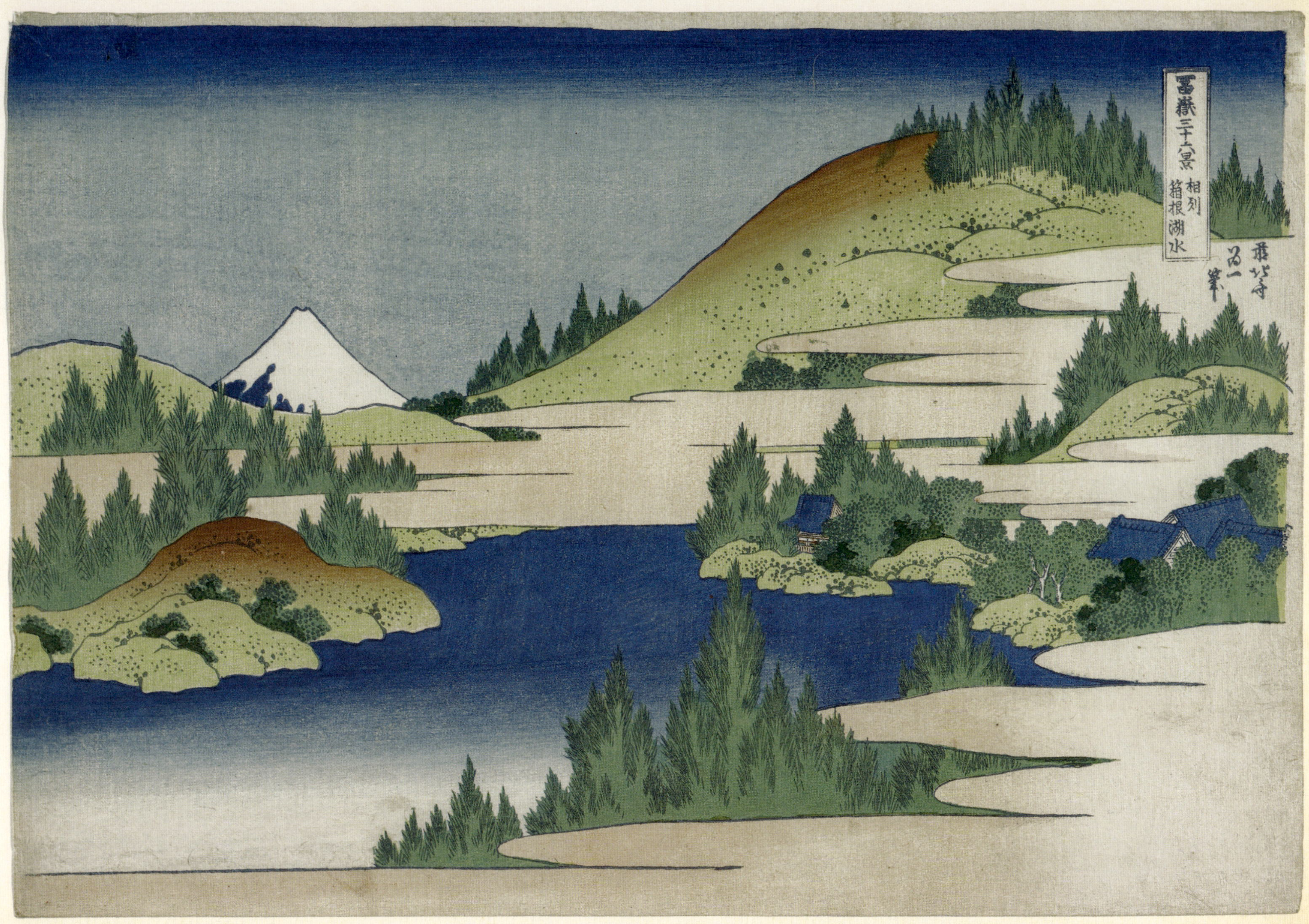
冨嶽三十六景
相刕箱根湖水
前北斎為一筆

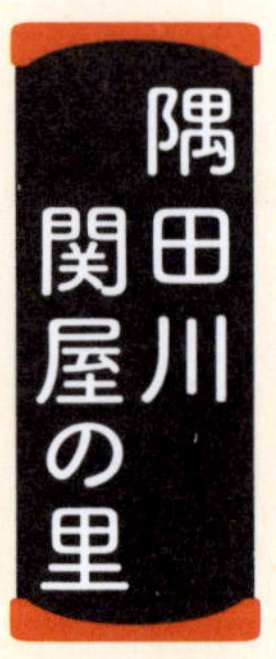

Sekiya Village on the Sumida River

Sumidagawa Sekiya No Sato

Three messengers on horseback gallop out of the village along a winding road, the one furthest away headed straight at Fuji; these are the protagonists of this dynamically-charged print. A tree in the middle of the print extends its branches as if gesturing toward the mountain, framing it together with a second tree on the right. The repetition of the three horseback riders along the windy road conjures up the sequenced dynamism of Futurist art, and also juxtaposes the statuesque stillness of the ancient mountain in the distance. A red Fuji is illuminated by the sunrise as the wispy mists of dawn are dissipating.

On the wall of a building on the right, posted bulletins announce official proclamations and injunctions. During the Edo period, an efficient system of communication existed using messengers on foot (*hikyaku*) and on horseback (*hayauma*). These official carriers had such priority and authority that no one could interfere with them. The horsemen in the print were probably government messengers. Hokusai draws on his extensive studies of human and animal movements to convincingly depict the motion of the riders.

The Sumida is a relatively short river that originates in the Kanto Mountains and flows through the eastern part of Tokyo from north to south, connecting a network of canals that flow into Tokyo Bay. Now, as in the Edo period, the river is integral to the life of the city, and along its shop-filled shores one can admire the spring cherry blossoms (*hanami*) and the summer fireworks (*hanabi*). Sekiya, a village located north of Edo, was famous for its beautiful landscapes.

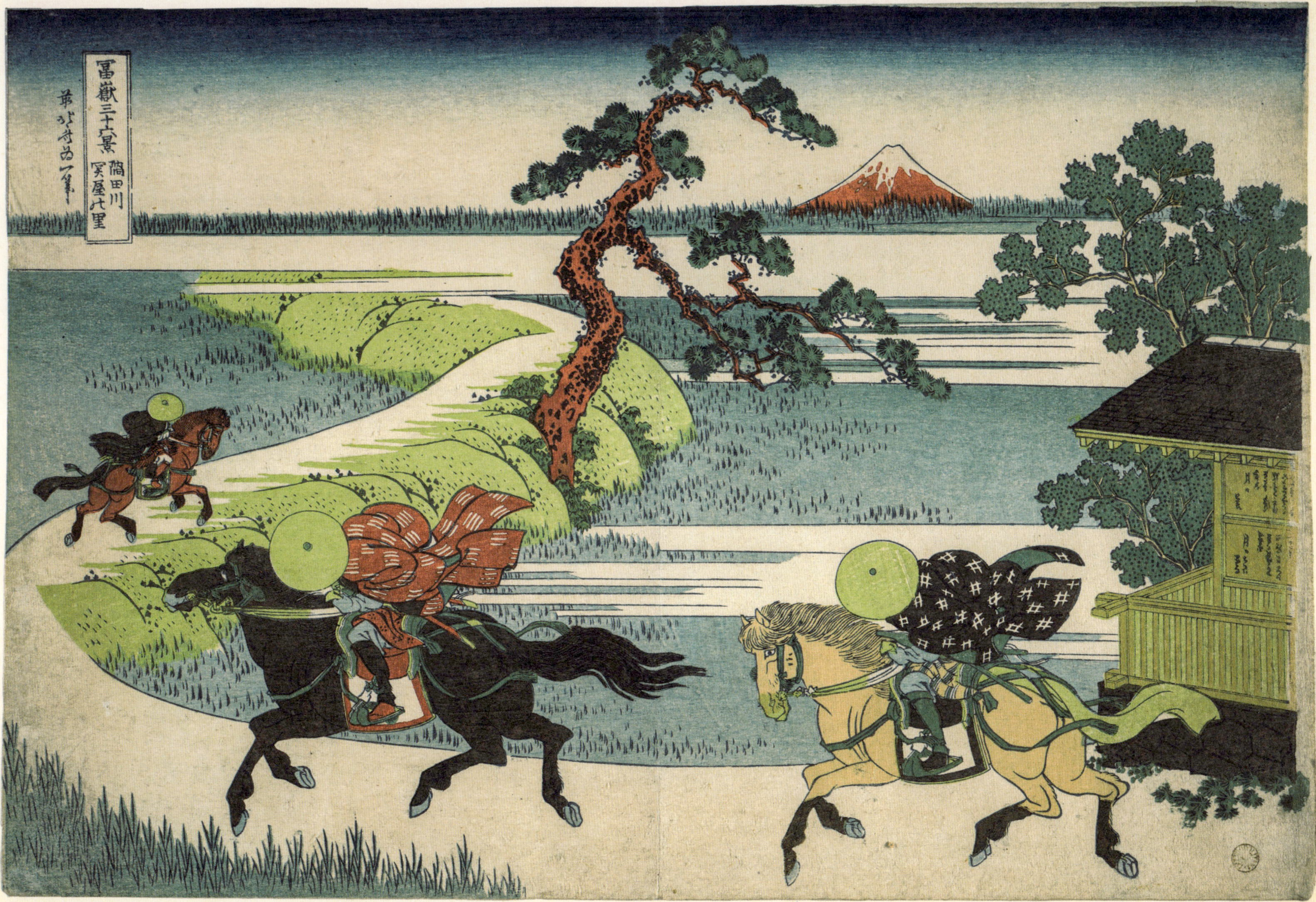

冨嶽三十六景　隅田川関屋の里
前北斎為一筆

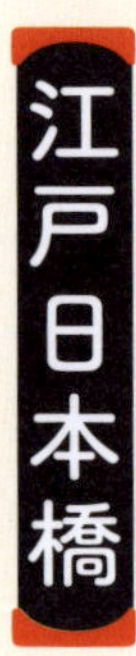

Nihonbashi in Edo

Edo Nihonbashi

Built in 1602, the Nihonbashi (literally "Japan Bridge") was an arched wooden bridge across the Kanda River, one of the several streams that flowed into the Sumida River in Edo. In Hokusai's time, it was the city's central point and most important crossroad as the starting point of the Gokaido, the five roadways that ran through Japan: Tokaido, Nakasendo, Koshu Kaido, Oshu Kaido and Nikko Kaido. For this reason, and because of its distinctive shape, it became a symbol of the capital. Within the city of Edo, a network of rivers and canals facilitated the transport of goods and people. The banks of these rivers were lined with shops, warehouses and residences. This print shows the back of the warehouses, where boats docked to load and unload goods. On the walls at right, the logos of several famous shops can be seen.

In this depiction of the commercial district around this famous bridge, Hokusai shows his mastery of Western perspective—the vanishing point converging on another bridge, above which towers the *shogun's* residence (now the imperial palace) with Fuji to its left. The artist exhibits remarkable originality in the way he crops the bottom of the image so the guardrails of the bridge are barely visible above the frenetic throng of goods and people. This close-up gives the print a profound sense of depth and meaning. The boats on the river are also full of commercial activity. Once again, Hokusai contrasts the frenzy of human affairs with the tranquility of ancient Fuji.

Rebuilt several times since the 17th century, the current bridge was built in stone in 1911. Today, Nihonbashi is the business center of Tokyo and houses many banks, shops and department stores.

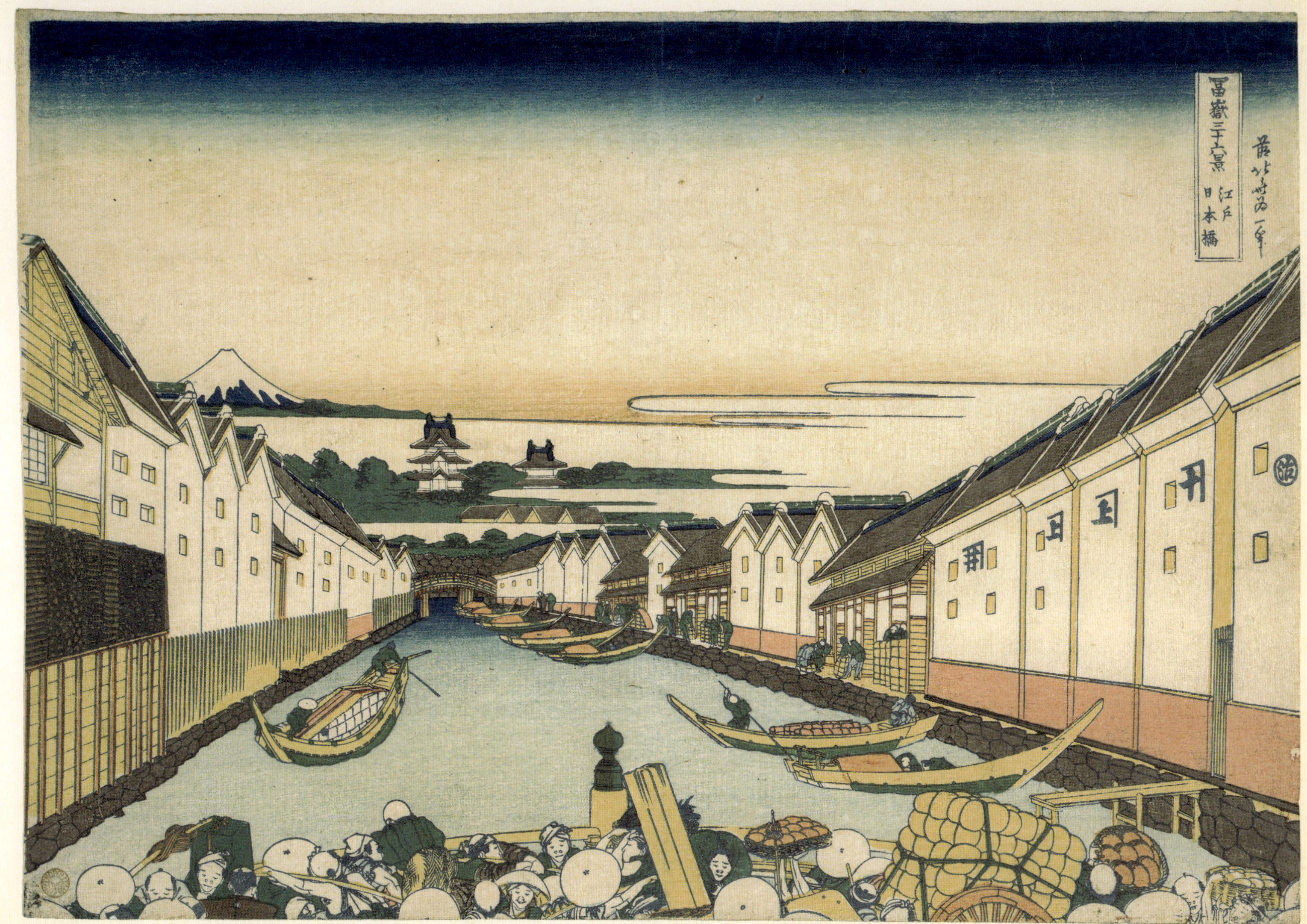
冨嶽三十六景　江戸　日本橋
葛飾北斎画の一筆

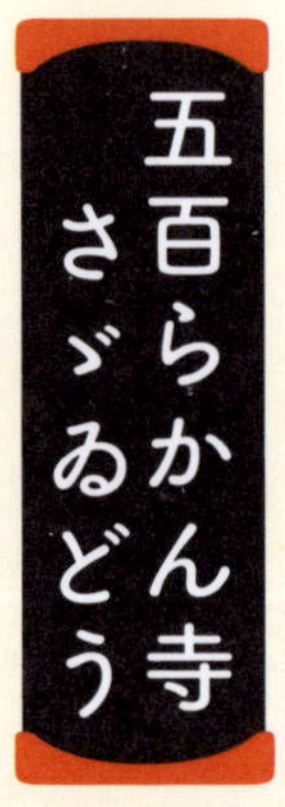

Sazai Hall at the Temple of the Five Hundred Arhats

Gohyaku Rakanji Sazaido

A group of visitors at the temple admire the view from the terrace. On the right, two porters sit next to the luggage they are carrying. On the left, a man points his finger toward the mountain. Another man on the right, nonchalantly wiping his head with a handkerchief, glances toward us over his shoulder, as if reaching beyond the print and inviting us to join the group's scenic viewing.

Fuji is almost perfectly centered in the picture, framed by the horizontal and vertical lines of the terrace. Far in the distance to the right of the volcano, one can see a row of wooden poles, likely scaffolding for construction. Serving almost as a vanishing point, it is clearly much closer to Fuji and attempts to imitate the mountain's shape. The light colors of the visitors' clothing suggest that it is summer.

The Sazai Hall (literally "turban-shell tower," referencing a type of Japanese clam that resembles the building's distinctive spiral staircase) is a three-story tower built in 1695. It served as a temple dedicated to the five hundred *rakan* (or *arhat* in original Sanskrit), who were disciples of Buddha and the protectors of Buddhist law. The spiral staircase of the temple opened up to this terrace where visitors could enjoy a stunning view of Fuji across the Sumida River.

The temple is located in the Meguro district of Tokyo and can still be visited today. Many of the original 500 statues are still there, all of which were made by the sculptor-king Shoun Genkei between 1691 and 1710.

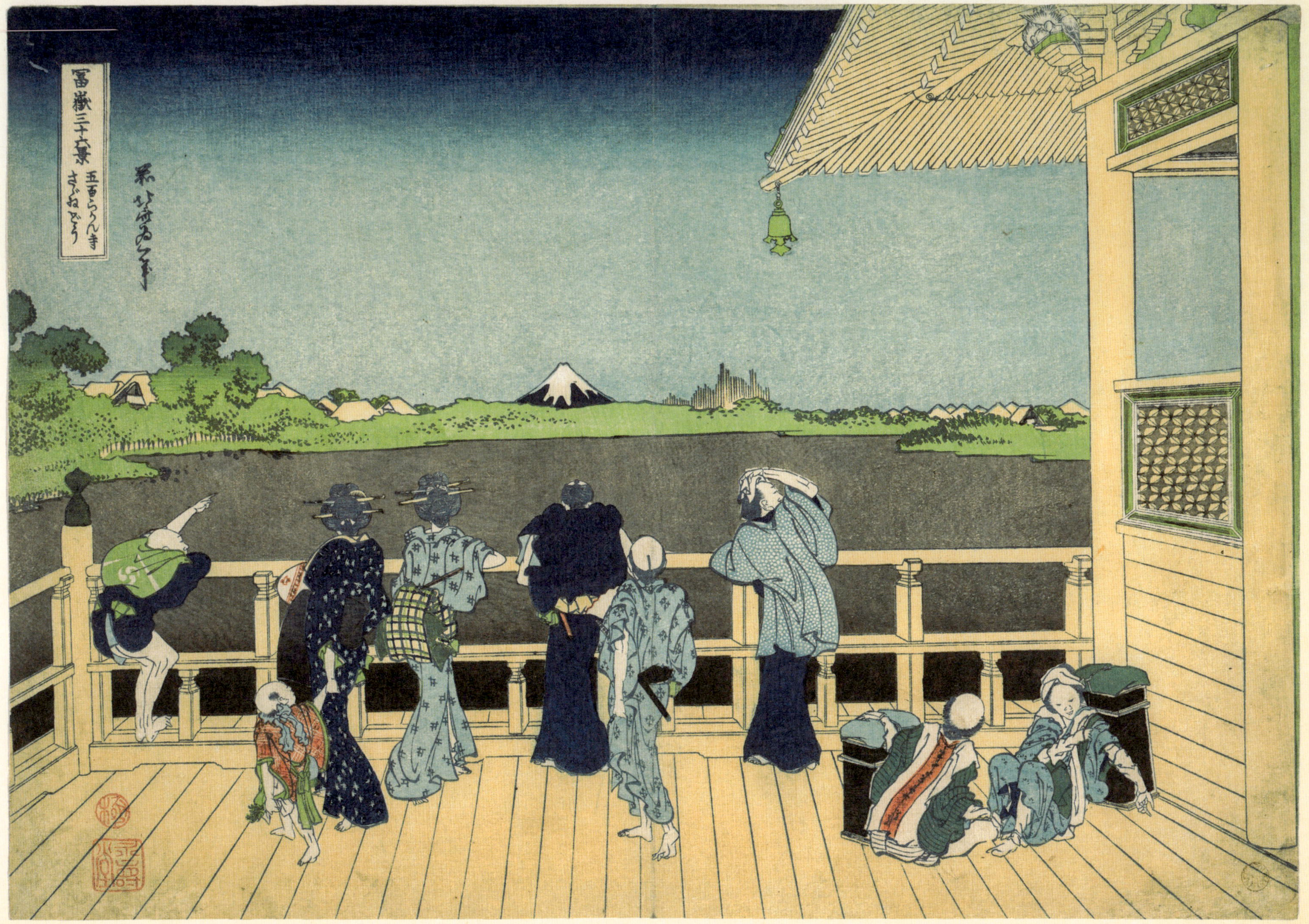

The Waterwheel at Onden

Onden No Suisha

The eponymous wheel of the print gushes water into a wooden channel that cuts horizontally across the scene. On one side of the waterway are two women—one holds a basket, the other a bucket—as a child drags a turtle on a leash (the same animal as in print #13). On the other side, two men are bringing sacks of rice to be milled. Each of the characters minds their own business, seemingly oblivious to the presence of Fuji.

The composition creates equilibrium out of a dance of geometric lines. Hokusai masterfully integrates each shape: the triangle of Fuji, the circle of the wheel, the parallel lines of the channel of water, and the cloud-like shapes of its flow. Like waves rolling downstream, Hokusai once again displays his talent for depicting water in motion.

During Hokusai's time in Edo, rice mills were powered by the waters of the Shibuya River in Onden, then a rural agricultural area. Onden was in what is today the area between Harajuku and Aoyama in Tokyo, a lively neighborhood full of clubs, popular cafés, and elegant shops where young people buy and wear the latest fashions.

Onden was also the name of the largest tributary of the Shibuya River. Today, these water channels are still visible in patches, though most of them flow underneath the asphalt. At the time, there were numerous watermills for grinding rice and the populace used the streams for washing food and clothes.

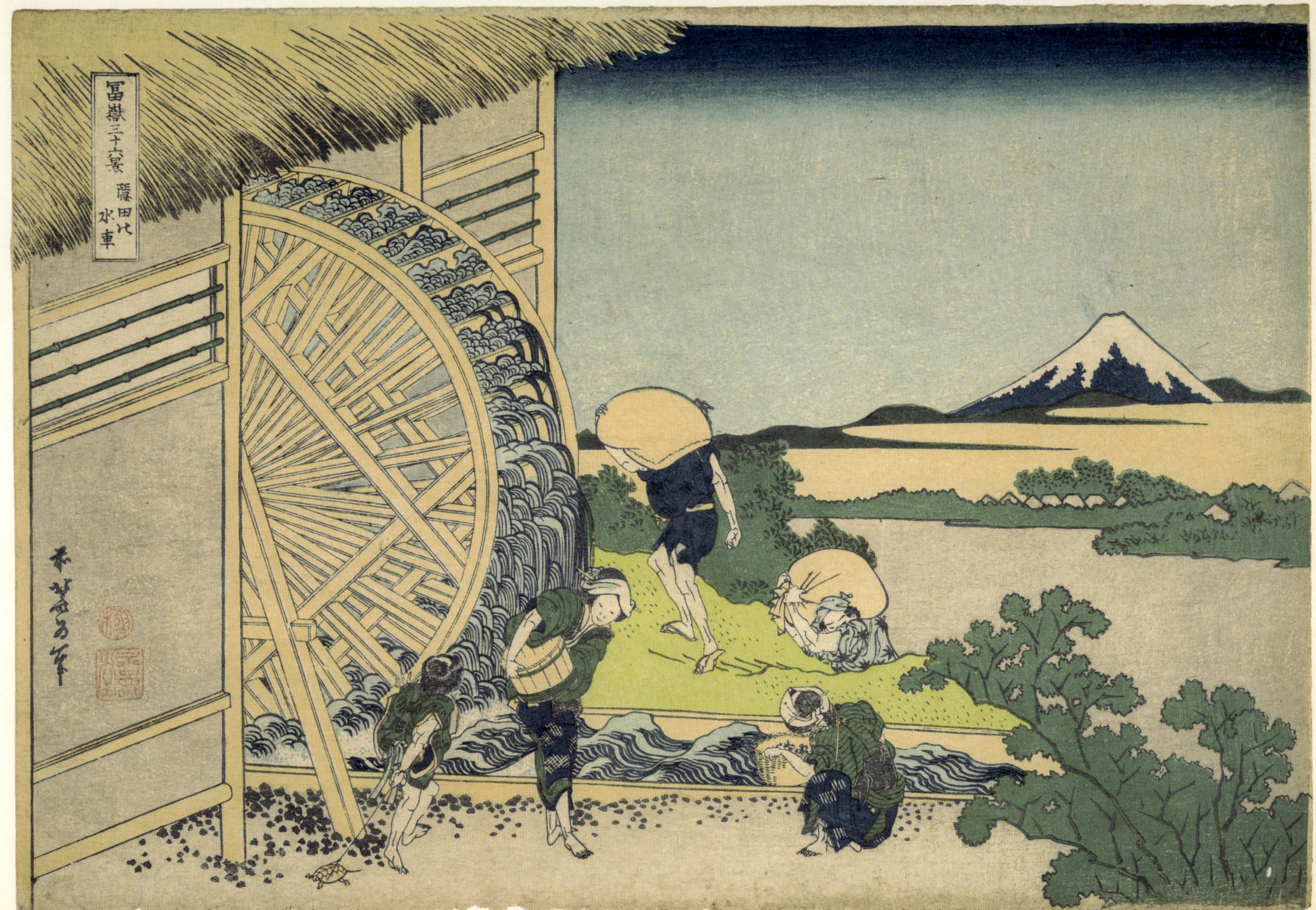

冨嶽三十六景　隱田水車
前北斎為一筆

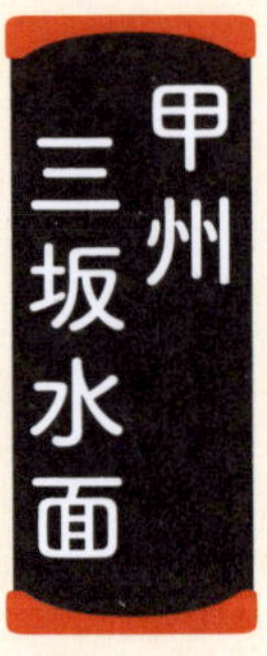

Reflection in the Lake at Misaka in Kai Province

Koshu Misaka Suimen

In this print Hokusai succeeds in representing Fuji not merely in space but also in time. Towering above the thatched-roof village and forest that populate the center of the image, the mountain is reflected in Lake Kawaguchi. A lone boat points toward Fuji—not the physical mountain, but its ethereal mirror-image. This replica, snow-covered and devoid of ridges, presents the volcano as it is popularly imagined, even though the print itself is set in summer or early autumn and shows the mountain naked and rough.

The reflection, the focal point of the print, captures Fuji's dual nature, physical and spiritual at the same time. The composition displays a perfect balance, the two versions of the mountain framed on either side by gentle hills and soft lines. The fisherman's boat gives the image a sense of depth and motion.

From the Misaka Pass north of Fuji, there are unobstructed panoramic views of Lake Kawaguchi and the mountain. In the title, Hokusai names the lake after the pass. As can be seen from the print, the northern side of the mountain has a more jagged and harsh appearance.

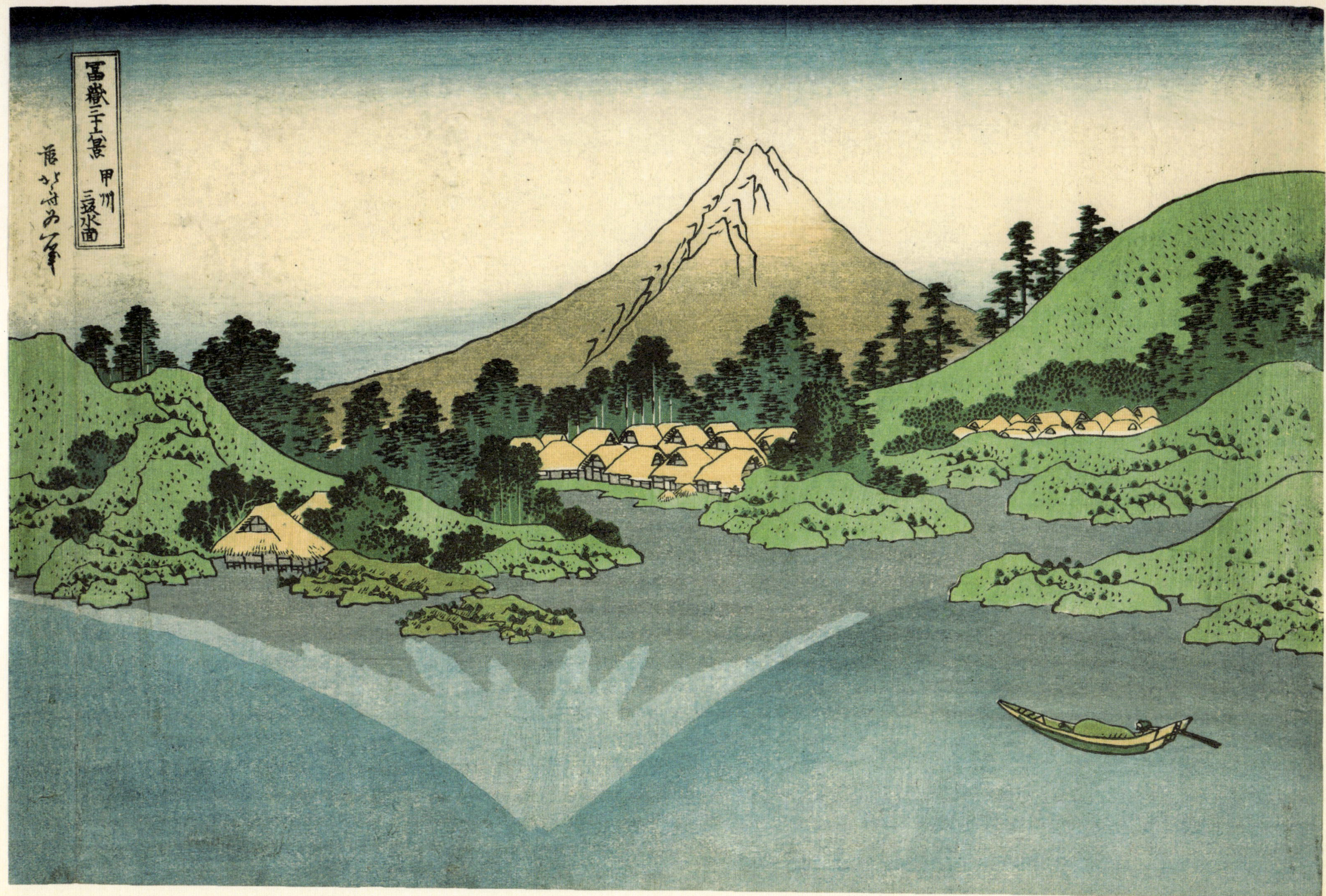

冨嶽三十六景　甲州三坂水面
前北斎為一筆

Once again, in his later series *One Hundred Views of Mount Fuji* (*Fugaku hyakkei*), we find an interesting parallel. Print #20—*Fuji on the Face of a Paddy* (*Tanomo no Fuji*), seen here at the right, shows only the reflection of the mountain in a pond. A flock of geese add movement and life to an otherwise static image. Some of them, fixed to the ground on the right, seem to be looking at the peak of Fuji, hidden from us, while those in flight on the left seem headed toward it.

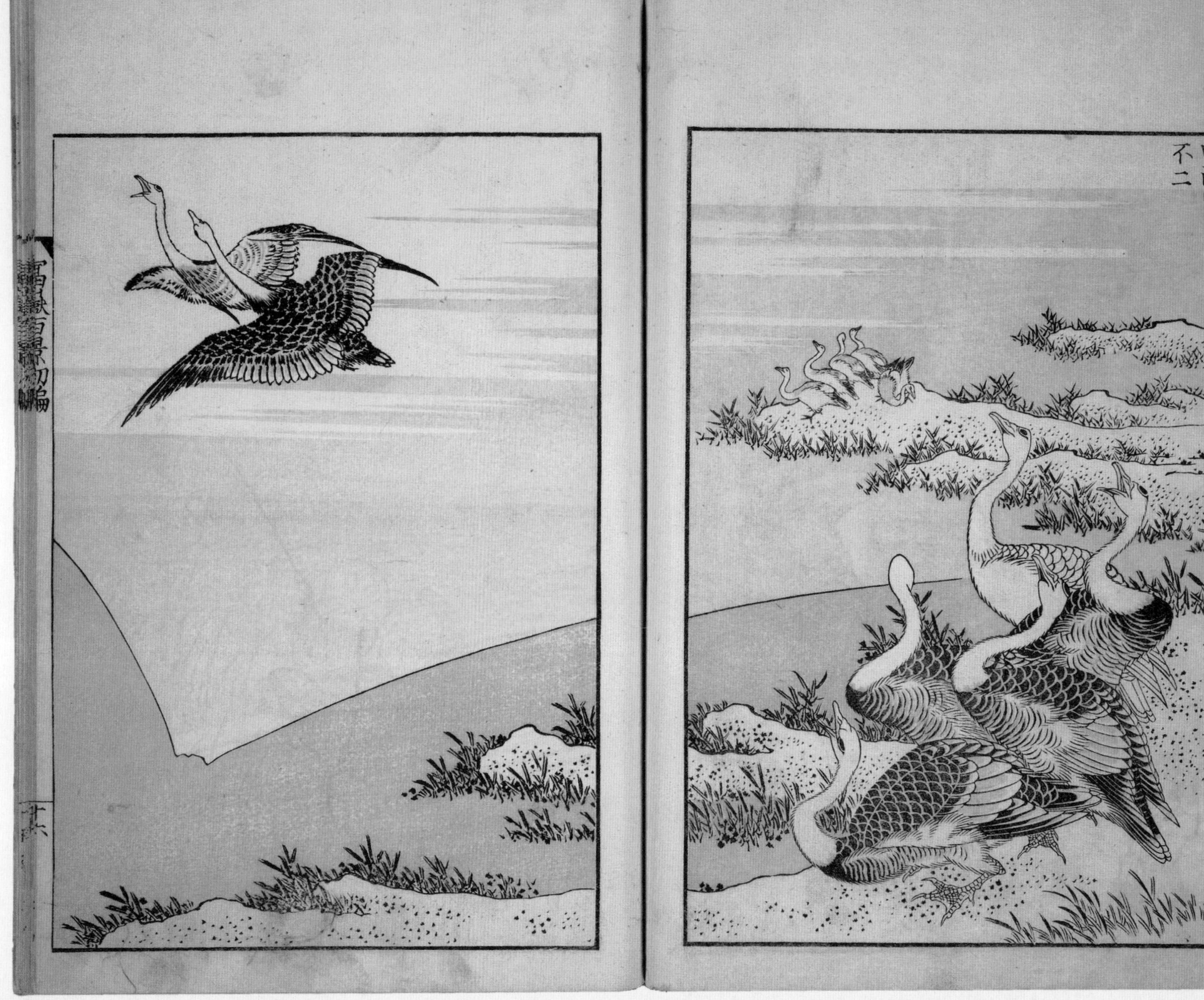

田面の不二
富嶽百景初編
江仙

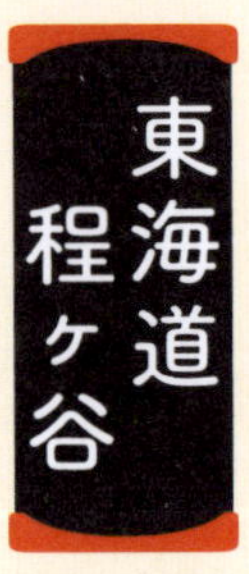

Hodogaya on the Tokaido

Tokaido Hodogaya

Near Hodogaya, the fourth post station on the Tokaido, there was a path lined with tall pine trees. The contortions of the trees are loosely imitated by the ensemble of travelers that Hokusai introduces to the scene. On the right, a wandering monk, wearing a straw hat and holding a bamboo flute, heads toward a shrine. In the middle, a servant leads a horse-mounted traveler. On the left, two porters carrying a woman in a palanquin have stopped to rest; one porter is wiping off his sweat while the other is tying his sandal.

The triangular shape formed by the man on the horse, his hat serving as the "summit" and his horse's front and back sloping downwards, echo the silhouette of Fuji, as do the branches of the pines above. The horse's saddle belt bears the mark 壽 (*ju*) of the publisher Eijudo (similar references are found in prints #23, 26, 37, 40, 45).

The man in the middle points his staff toward the sacred mountain is the only one facing in its direction. The steep hill on the right is terraced with a religious image carved into the rock face. The print as a whole exudes a feeling of great dynamism, balanced by the firm and serene presence of Fuji.

Hodogaya was located between Musashi in Edo Province and Sagami Province to the west. It was said that here, where the road stretches into a beautiful boulevard lined with pine trees on both sides, travelers heading west felt the sensation of having finally left the capital behind. Hodogaya was once a small fishing village but is today part of the large city of Yokohama.

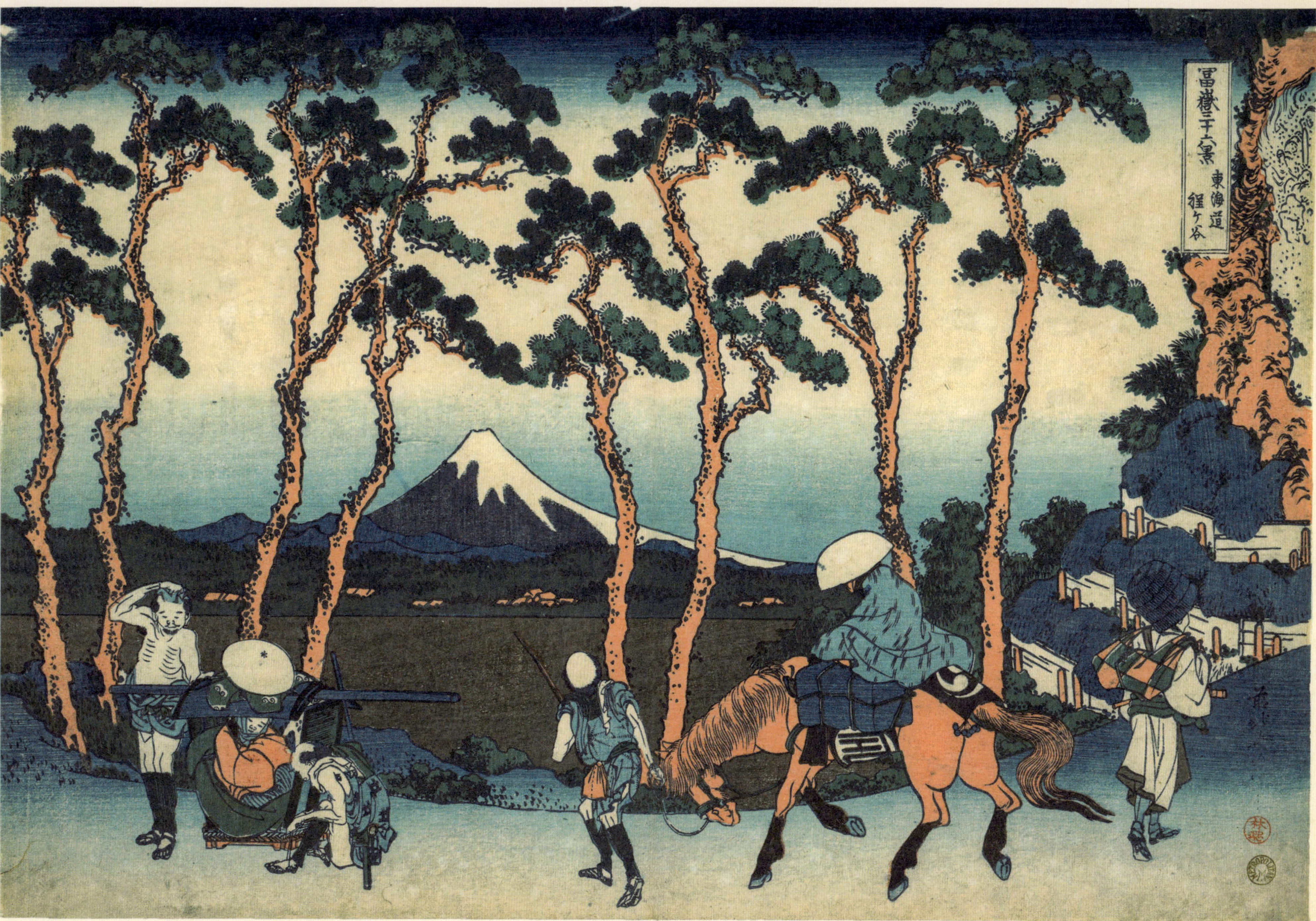

冨嶽三十六景
東海道
程ケ谷

Tatekawa in Honjo

Honjo Tatekawa

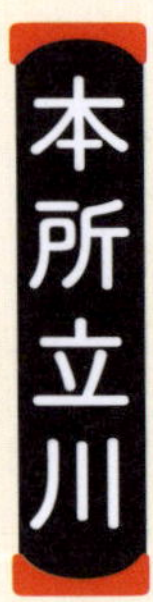

This is the first of the ten additional prints that were added by popular demand after the exceptional success of the original thirty-six. Three men are busily constructing a large building on the banks of the Tatekawa River (near Asakusa, Tokyo) in Honjo, a district known for its timber yards. Here, the Tatekawa, a small river flowing from west to east, converges into the Sumida River at Ryogoku Bridge.

On the lower right, some of the wooden boards bear the inscriptions: "Sawmill of Nishimura" (the name of the series' publisher), the publisher's address, "material for Eijudo" and "a new edition of the complete *Thirty-six Views of Fuji.*"

The composition is full of straight lines that stand in contrast to the torqued motions of the men at work. Their exaggerated forms are reminiscent of the studies on movement that Hokusai recorded in large numbers in his fifteen *Manga* sketchbooks (three of which were published posthumously).

On the far right, Fuji is partially hidden by construction materials, a decision probably made by the artist in order not to make Fuji's presence immediately obvious in the first addition to the original series. Hokusai was a master of both meticulous realism and abstraction. Here, he expresses his love of detail with intricate renderings of the timber yards and construction site.

Honjo, now in the Sumida district of Tokyo, developed when many timber merchants settled in the area after the great Meireki fire of 1657.

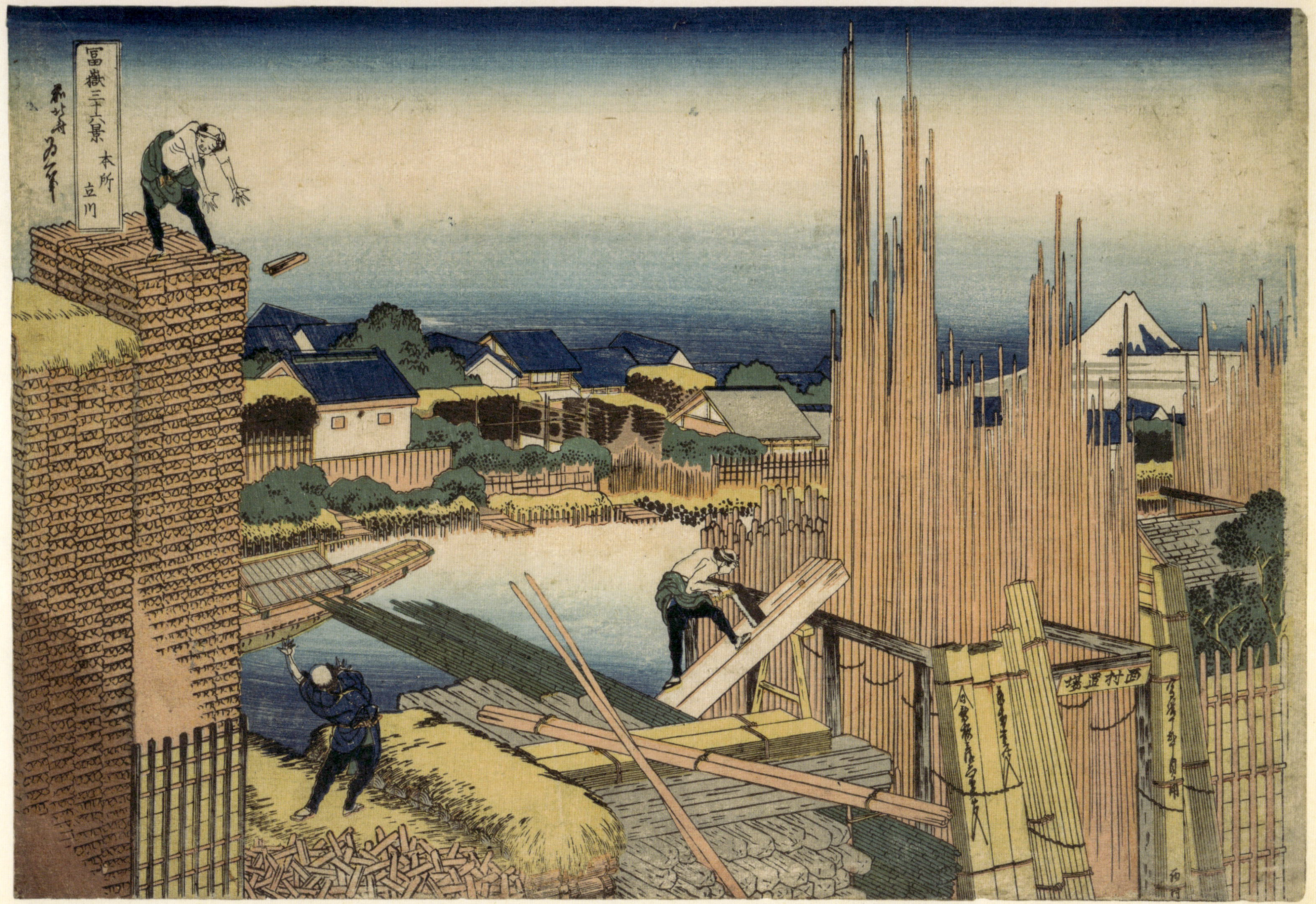

冨嶽三十六景　本所立川
前北斎為一筆

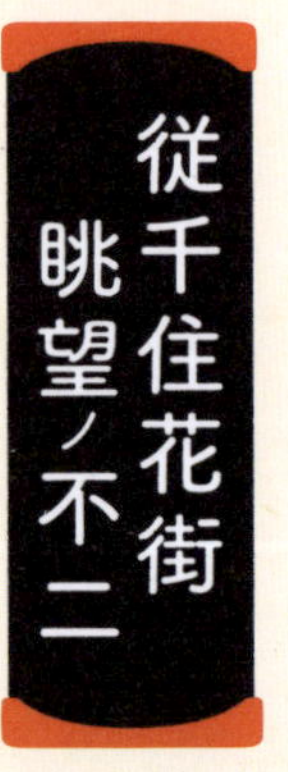

38

Fuji Seen in the Distance
from the Senju Pleasure Quarter

Senju Kagai Yori Chobo No Fuji

On an autumn day, the entourage of a *daimyo* (feudal lord) leaves Edo to begin their long journey to their home province. *Daimyo* were required by the system of *sankin kotai* to alternate their residence between the capital and their own domain every year.

Numbering up to two thousand people, a retinue on the move was a spectacle. The feudal lord's men can be seen each carrying two swords, one short and one long, reserved only for samurai; their scarlet bags conceal firearms. On the left, tips of spears can be spotted behind the tree branches. The marching men are entering a rest stop where straw sandals hang from the rafters. Several of the men, particularly the leftmost one who rests his hand on his forehead, turn their gaze toward Fuji; maybe they are pondering the pleasures they are leaving behind.

Surrounded by wooden fences, the Senju pleasure quarter depicted in the background gives the print its name. Unlike the more famous Yoshiwara pleasure quarter, Senju was operated in private without official government sanction.

The parade and Senju are separated by a paddy field where two women rest on an embankment to see the men off. Above them, Fuji reigns from a central position far in the distance. The harvested fields and snow on Fuji's summit suggest that it is autumn.

Clouds or fog in the style of *suyari gasumi* paintings, moving toward the center from either flank, were often used in Japanese art to indicate a change of place or time. Hokusai uses this technique to direct our gaze to specific points throughout the image.

One of the five great roadways, the Nikko Kaido ran northeast of Edo to connect the capital with the shrine of Nikko; Senju was the first station on its route. Today it is located in Adachi, north of Tokyo, but its view of Mount Fuji is now blocked by numerous buildings.

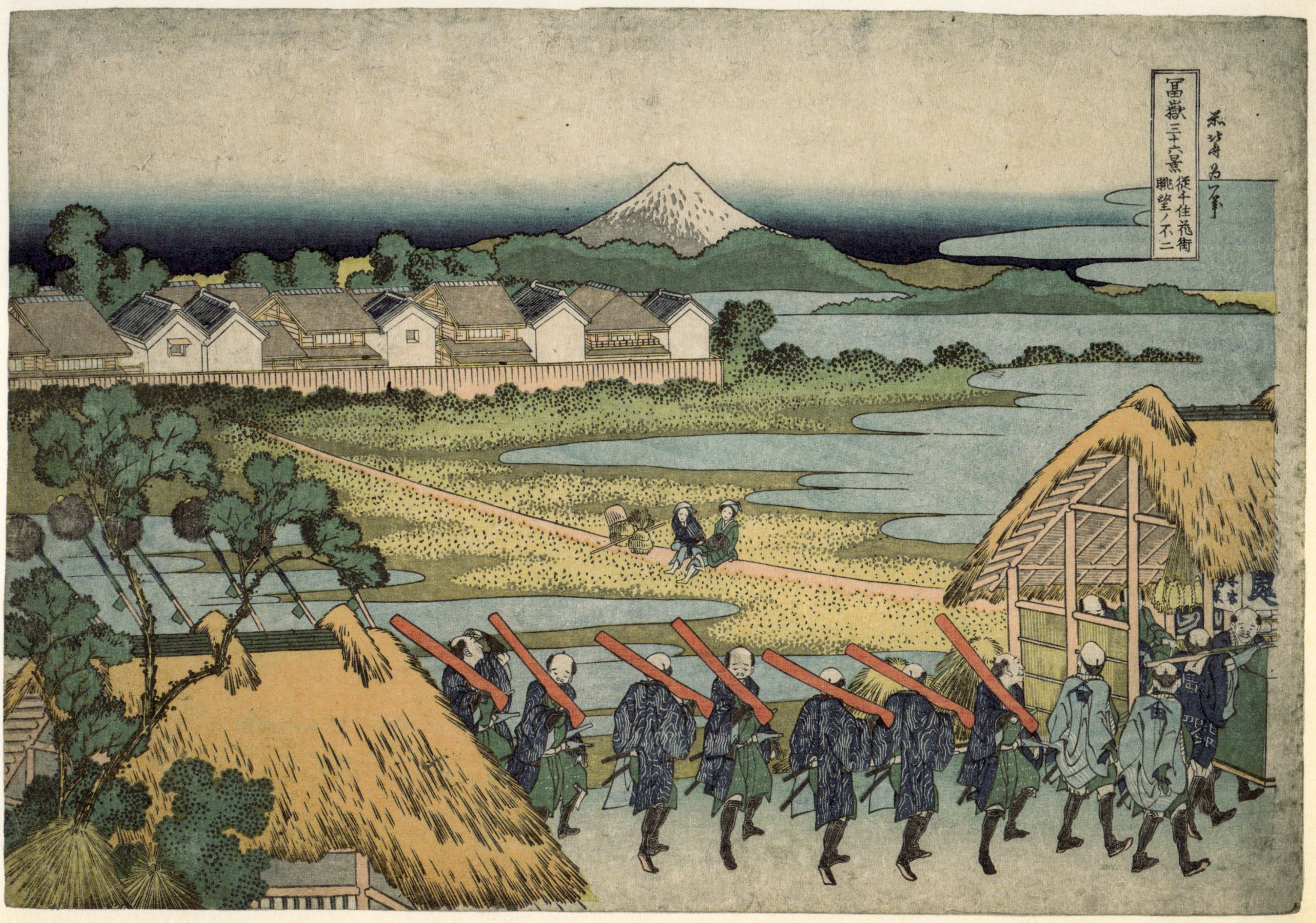

冨嶽三十六景 従千住花街眺望ノ不二
前北斎為一筆

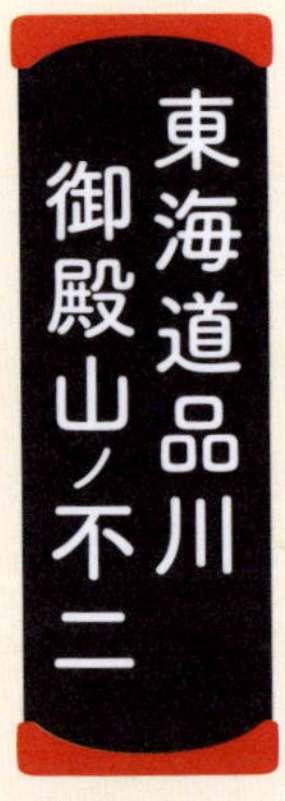

39

Fuji from Gotenyama at Shinagawa on the Tokaido

Tokaido Shinagawa Gotenyama No Fuji

A group of people gather to admire the blossoming cherry trees in the *hanami* tradition. As in other compositions, Fuji appears in the distance while the foreground is animated by the presence of blossoming trees and an array of characters. Among them are samurai and ordinary citizens, a trio picnicking on mats laid on the ground, women carrying children on their shoulders, and people inside a drinking establishment. Men are dancing, fans twirling in their hands; perhaps they are already drunk. Far away on the right, people stroll along the shore of Tokyo Bay.

Among the people in the scene, no one seems to be paying any attention to the volcano or even the cherry trees. A popular saying goes *hana yori dango* ("[sweet] rice cakes are better than flowers"): eating is more fun than looking at flowers. Hokusai interpreted the popular saying with irony, but without detracting from the beauty of the scene.

This is among Hokusai's most detailed compositions and one of the richest in energy. The bustle and emotion of the people, but also the soft color of the flowers, lends levity and liveliness to the image.

The mountain is seen across Sagami Bay from Gotenyama, a hill located north of Shinagawa, which is now a district in southeastern Tokyo. Gotenyama was a popular spot for picnics because of its beautiful view of the ocean and Fuji, surrounded by cherry trees that date back to the Kanbun period (1661–1672). Shinagawa was the first of the fifty-three Tokaido stations after the starting point at Nihonbashi.

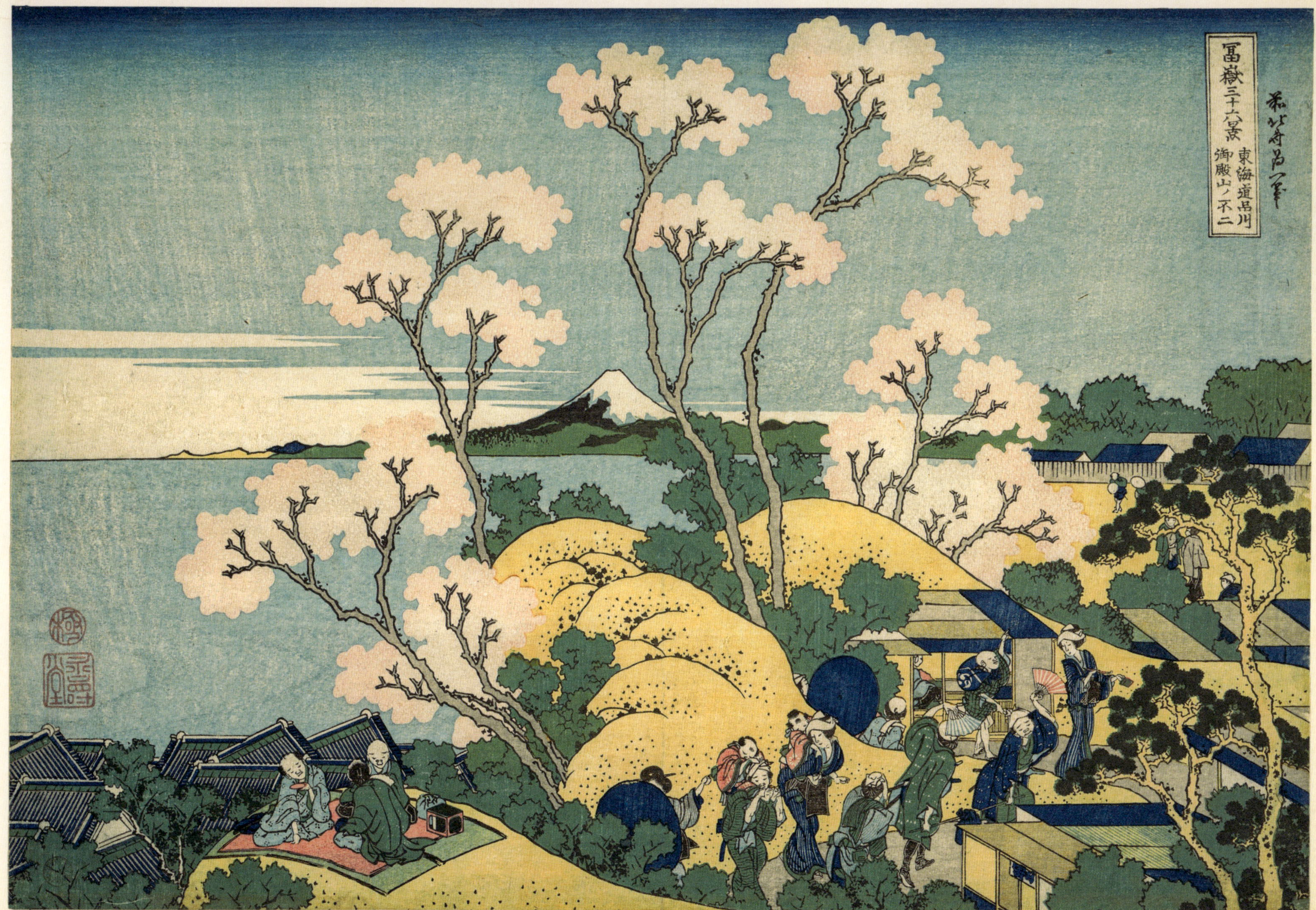
冨嶽三十六景　東海道品川
御殿山ノ不二
前北斎為一筆

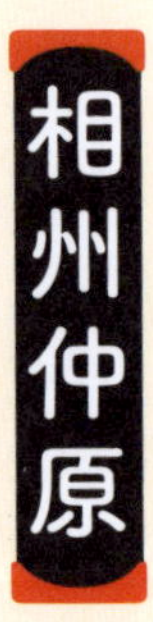

40

Nakahara in Sagami Province

Soshu Nakahara

Hokusai demonstrates a boundless capacity for compositional innovation and originality in depicting human diversity, even when repeating the same general subjects. The shape of Fuji, occupying the upper third of this print, is mirrored in the lines of the bridge and the shape of the roof protruding from the lower right, as well as the cords that extend behind the hut. Bells are attached to these ropes in order to frighten the birds and keep them away from the water.

In the middle, travelers and locals traverse the bridge in a manner reminiscent of a kabuki stage and its *hanamichi* (a kind of platform stretching from the stage into the audience). A pilgrim lugs a portable shrine followed by a boy holding a closed umbrella; a peasant woman carries a child on her shoulders; a fisherman sifts through his fishing basket; a farmer laden with goods holds a bird whistle; another pilgrim with a portable shrine is accompanied by his shop assistant. The latter gazes toward Fuji. He wears a typical striped city kimono, the lower part tucked into the waist for easier movement. He carries an umbrella and a large bundle wrapped in a blue *furoshiki*. It bears a logo showing three swirling commas (*tomoe*) under a roof, another shape that evokes Fuji, but is also the mark of Hokusai's publisher, Eijudo. However, the most striking character is the woman on the bridge. Carrying a child on her back and a large wooden basket on her head filled with parcels of food for lunch, she simultaneously balances an iron kettle on the handle of her hoe.

This is one of Hokusai's most successful compositions despite its simplicity. The lower half of the print is characterized by a richness of detail that is offset by the simple lines and solid colors of the upper half.

Nakahara was in the Sagami Province, but is now in Hiratsuka, southwest of Tokyo. In the middle of the picture one can see the back of a shrine to the god Fudo. It points the way to Mount Oyama, visible in front of Fuji on the right. During the Edo period, this smaller mountain was a popular destination for devout Shintoists and Buddhists.

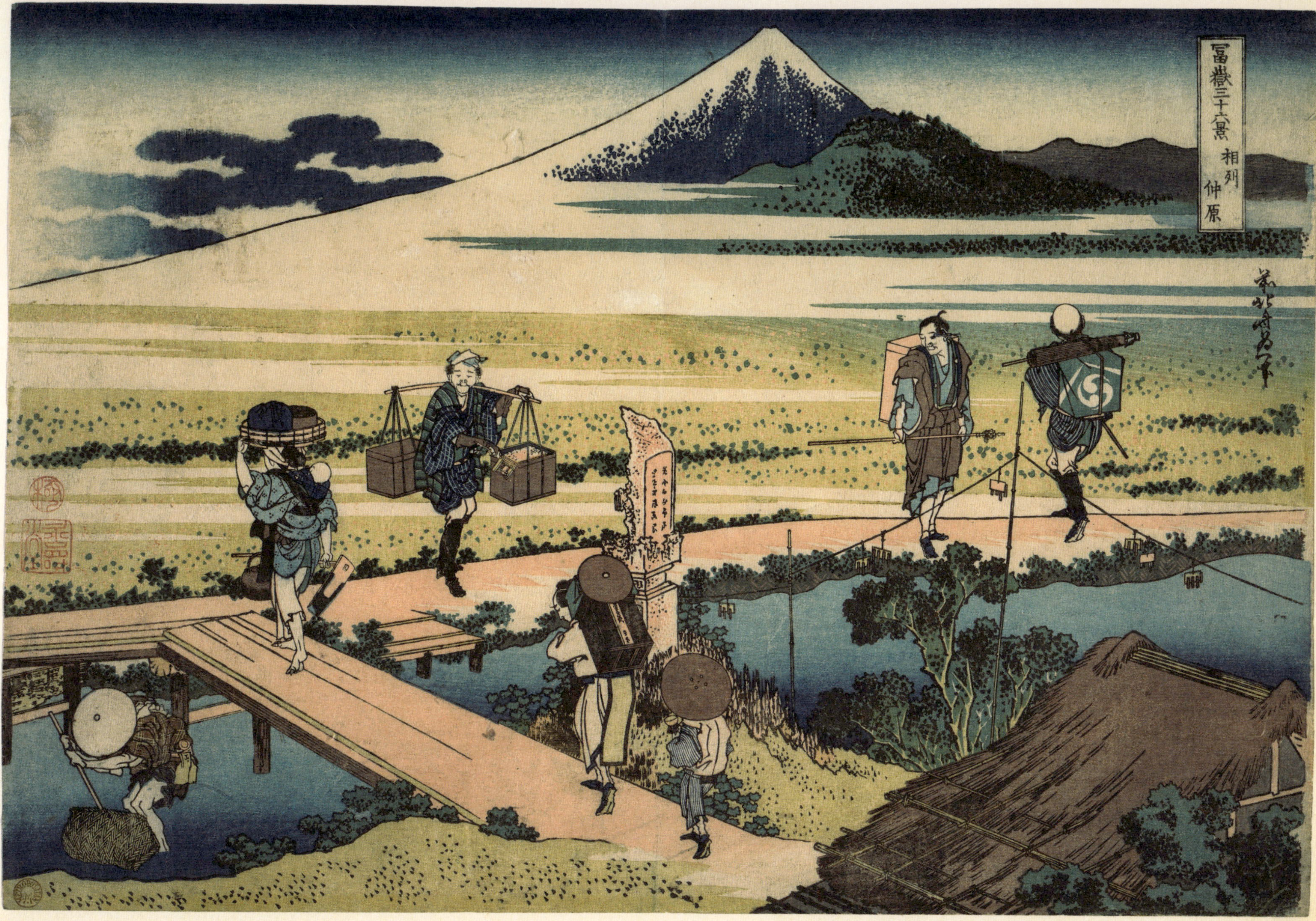
冨嶽三十六景 相州
仲原

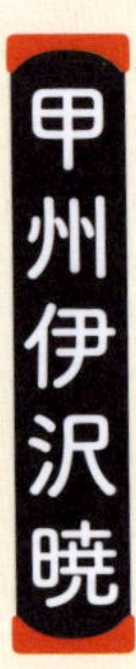

Dawn at Isawa in Kai Province

Koshu Isawa No Akatsuki

A group of travelers departs at the crack of dawn. They leave the village inns of Isawa and head for the bridge, whose structure fades into the mists and vegetation, but will hopefully guide them toward Fuji.

Isawa is a small town on the Fuefuki River to the west of Tokyo, in present-day Yamanashi Prefecture. In Hokusai's time, it was one of the stations on the Koshu Kaido (the road leading from Edo to Lake Suwa). Today, Isawa is a popular spa resort.

Fuji is seen here from "behind" (*ura Fuji*), i.e. from the north, and it seems disconnected from the earthly realm, as if inhabiting an idealized and spiritual space.

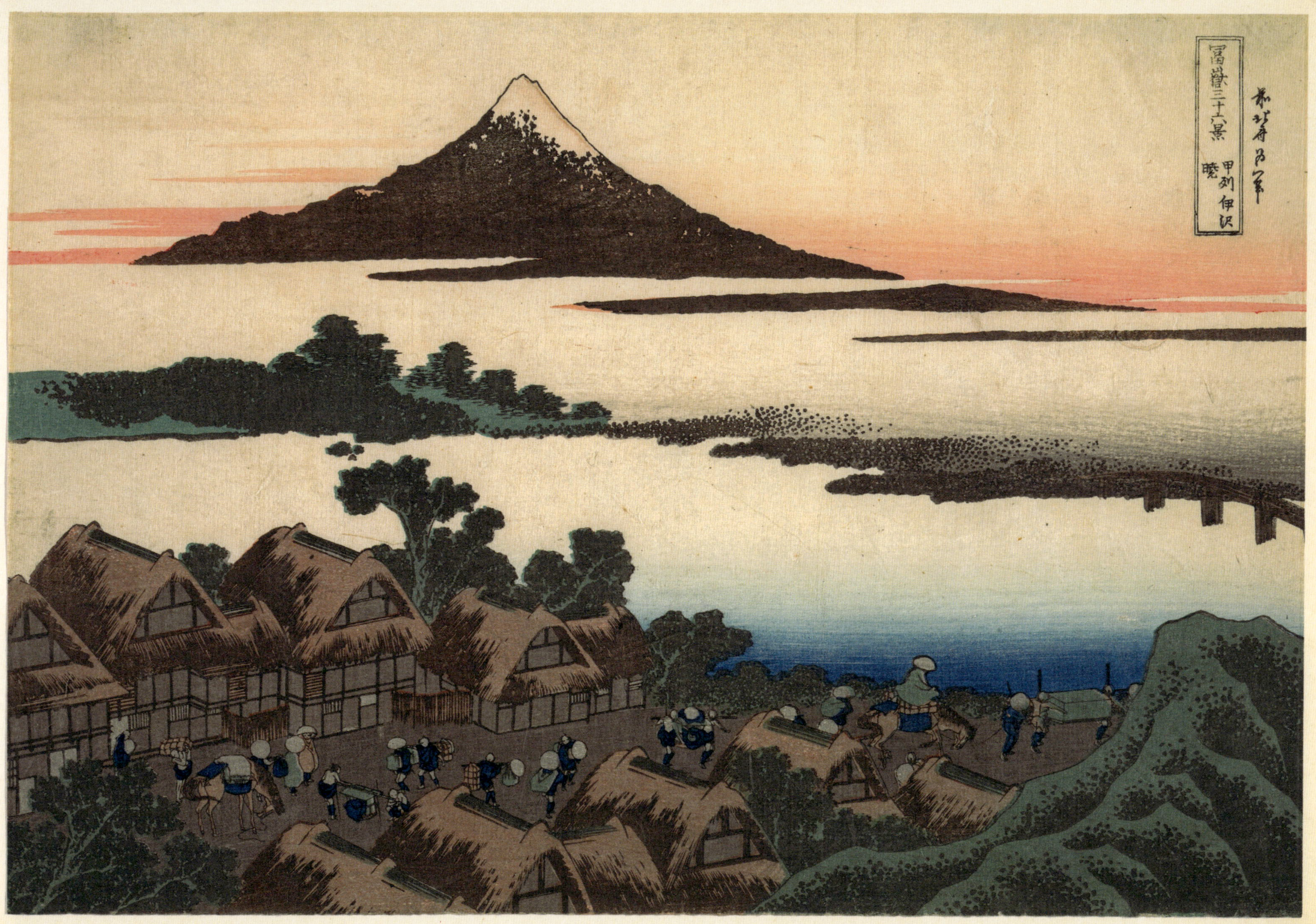
冨嶽三十六景
甲州伊沢
暁
前北斎為一筆

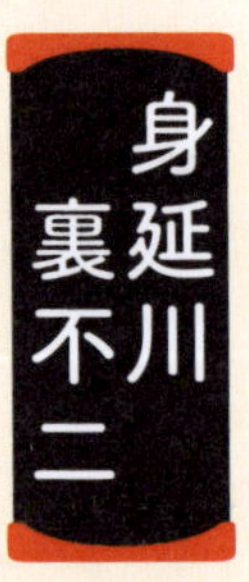

42

View of the Other Side
of Fuji from the Minobu River

Minobugawa Ura Fuji

This is another view of Fuji from the northern side (*ura Fuji*), known for its steep and rugged mien. In the foreground, we see another ensemble of travelers by now familiar to us: vendors, farmers, two horses and a palanquin hauled by two porters.

The landscape in the background is more dramatic than usual, both in form and color, and gives the impression of a remote mountainous region. Unlike in other prints, we are much closer to Fuji, largely hidden by two rugged peaks towering before it and calling to mind painted Chinese landscapes. Hokusai, like many other artists of the period, had studied Chinese painting through the *Mustard Seed Garden Manual of Painting* (*Kaishien gaden*), which had circulated in Japan since the 17th century.

The coarse character of the area is conveyed through curled, tense strokes, as well as intense shades of red and blue for the mountains and deep foreboding gray between the river and the low-lying clouds. The tree on the right acts almost like a third peak, directing our gaze toward Fuji. The rushing water of the Minobu River resemble folds of fabric that accentuate the rugged landscapes. The waves themselves consist of small colored dots, a technique used in other prints in the series.

This work is the only one to bear the words *"ura Fuji"* in its title. The road bordering this river leads to Kuonji, the main temple of the Nichiren Buddhist school. It is likely that some of the figures in the scene are journeying to the temple.

The "Minobu River" in the title is considered a mistake on the part of Hokusai. The river that flows near Minobu in Yamanashi Prefecture, is called Fuji and the Haya River is a branch that flows into it along this route.

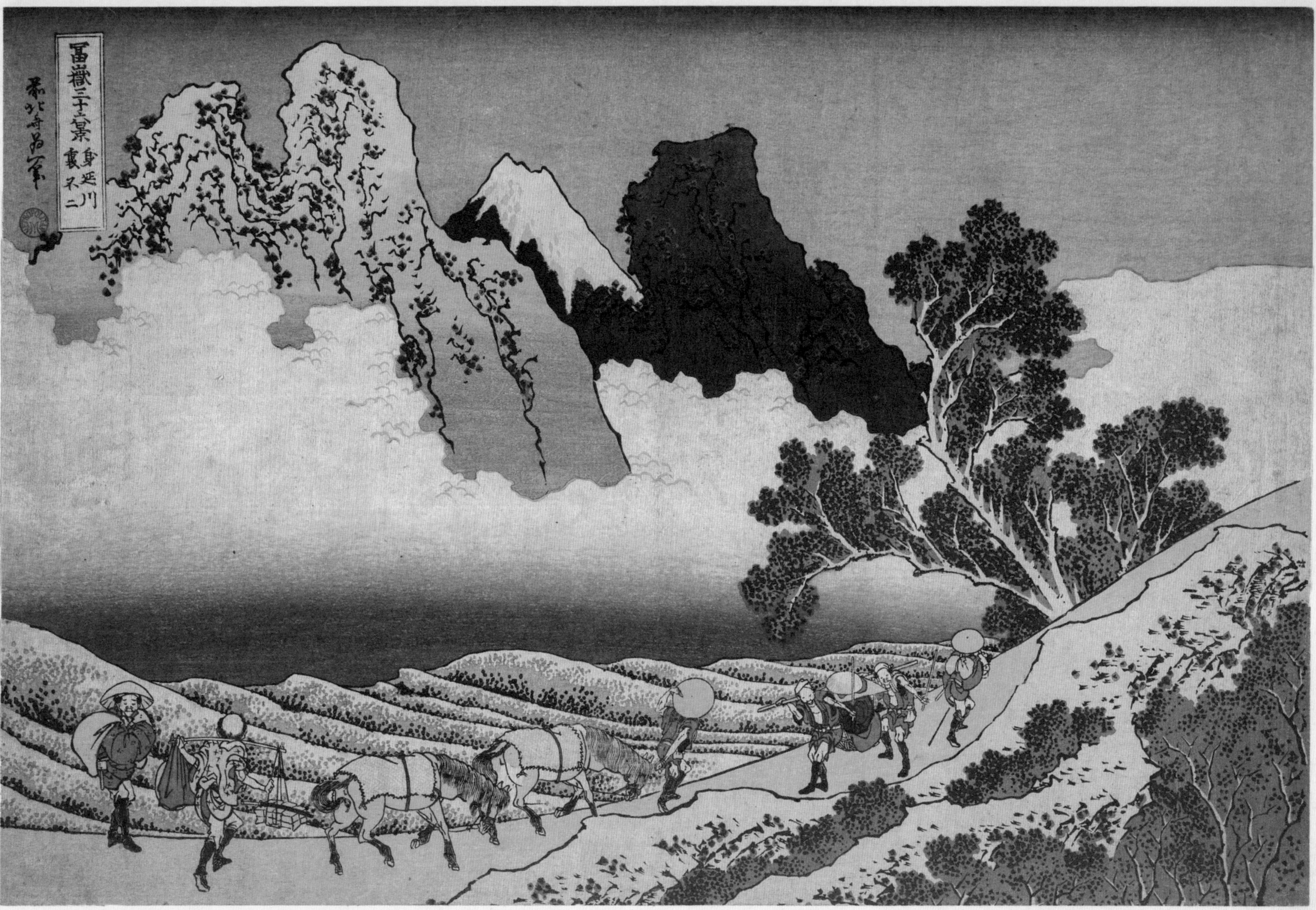
冨嶽三十六景
身延川
裏不二

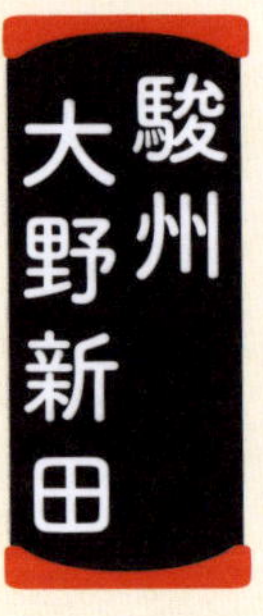

43

The New Fields at Ono in Suruga Province

Sunshu Ono Shinden

This print depicts the marshy rice fields at Ono, with mists rising from the wet grass as birds skim the surface of the water. Fuji towers above the fog, almost touching the upper edge of the print. The ethereal landscape in the background contrasts sharply with the human activity in the foreground, which captures a group of farmers returning home after a hard day of work. Several men walk along the edge of the damp paddy fields, leading oxen laden with reeds. Two are smoking pipes. On the left, two women carry bundles of grass on their backs.

The color scheme is simple: shades of blue and green dominate except for the pinkish sky on the right and the brown-red reeds and oxen.

Ono Shinden was an area that developed during the Edo period near the present-day town of Yoshiwara. Shinden, meaning "new fields", was a label given to newly cultivated lands. During the Edo period, the shogunate endeavored to expand agriculture to support the growing population and increase land taxes. Many swampy wild areas were thus reclaimed. Ono was one such area, located between the Hara and Yoshiwara stations on the Tokaido (14th and 15th stations).

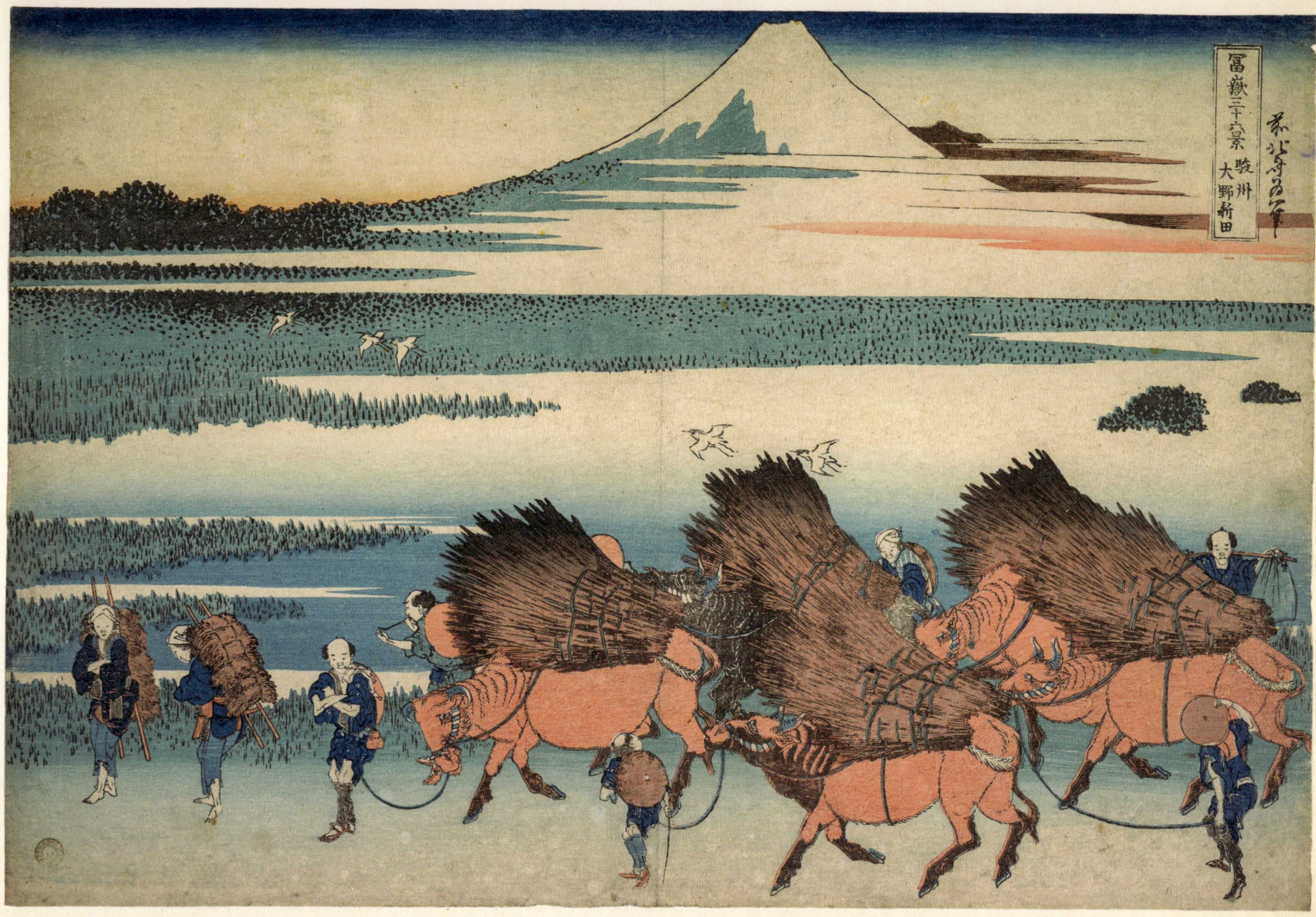
冨嶽三十六景　駿州　大野新田
前北斎為一筆

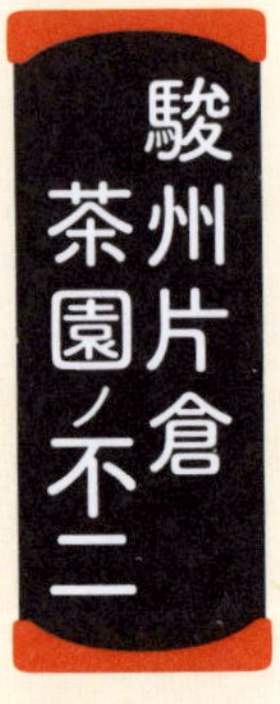

Fuji from the Katakura Tea Fields in Suruga

Sunshu Katakura Chaen No Fuji

Located in Shizuoka Prefecture, this area was known as Suruga until the end of the Edo period. It was famous for green tea production since at least the Muromachi period (1329–1573) and continues to produce and export tea to this day.

Hokusai here shows us a tea plantation, depicting its daily operations with his characteristic talent for detailing the movements and activities of people. Women stand and sit in rows picking tea leaves while men carry the leaves in baskets. One man packs tea into the baskets as others are hunched under the weight of a full haul; one man struggles to pull a skittish horse across a bridge; another inspects the hooves of a different one. The scene is rich in action and detail.

Fuji hovers on the horizon, above green tea fields and thatched roofs where gradients of yellow, green and brown create a sense of depth. The shape of the mountain is repeated several times at different sizes throughout the image: in the roofs of the houses and the winding paths along the waterways. Its presence percolates through the scene, exuding a sense of stability and calm.

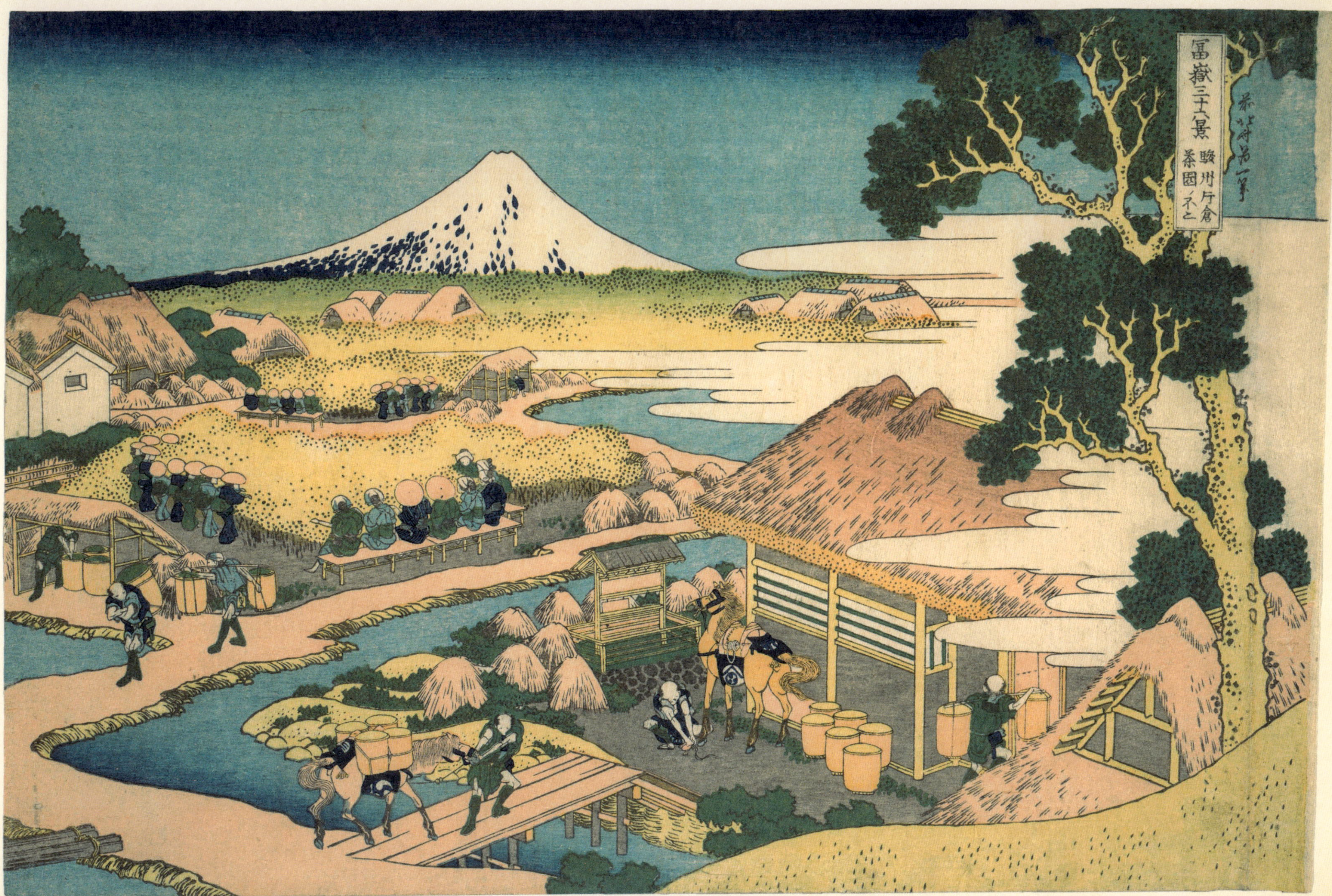

冨嶽三十六景
駿州片倉茶園ノ不二
前北斎為一筆

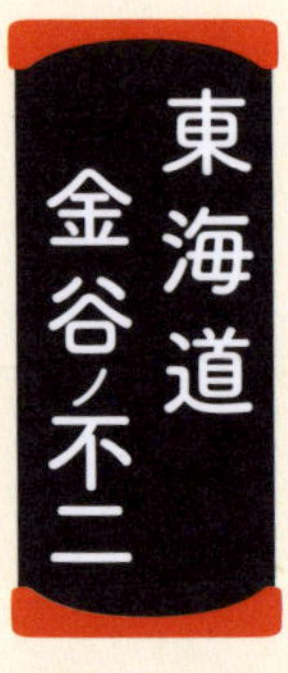

Fuji Seen from Kanaya on the Tokaido

Tokaido Kanaya No Fuji

Like the previous print, this one is rich in detail, but more focused in terms of movement and tension. Many travelers can be seen crossing the Oi River, located in present-day Shizuoka Prefecture. Ordinary travelers traverse the waters on the shoulders of chest-deep porters, while wealthier ones have hired teams to carry their palanquins and luggage on long stretchers. Prices varied depending on the depth of the river and the weather. Some are on their way into the river, others are halfway across. On the shore, porters are getting ready while other travelers continue their journey. On the bundled capes of a few travelers on the river, one can see the coat of arms of the publisher Nishimura. The flag in the village and the wrapped crate on the left display the characters 永 and 壽 respectively: 壽 (*kotobuki*, "happiness") may indicate the carriage of a woman who is en route to marry a man on the other side of the river, but it also alludes to Nishimura's shop, called Eijudo (永寿堂; 壽 is the archaic version of 寿).

Beyond the river, a small cluster of blossoming cherry trees announces the beginning of spring. The round embankments on the opposite shore are dams made of long bamboo baskets filled with gravel to reduce flooding. Fuji rises majestically behind. The town of Shimada can be glimpsed through the opening in the walls.

The Oi River was considered the most difficult obstacle to cross on the Tokaido because of its powerful currents. Nevertheless, the shogunate, for defensive reasons, decided not to build a bridge across the river.

The strong currents of the river are rendered with an aesthetic simplicity that is very different from the *The Great Wave* (#16), but nonetheless achieves great effect; the style harkens back to Hokusai's early prints where he experimented with shadow and perspective using Western *chiaroscuro*. Lines, dots and colors perfectly capture the motion of the waves as they dissipate into foam. The tangles of naked bodies and straw hats turning in every direction lends a visceral tone to the human activity, like a cacophony of voices. In the background of a scene so full of movement and danger, Fuji is a reassuring presence that all will go well.

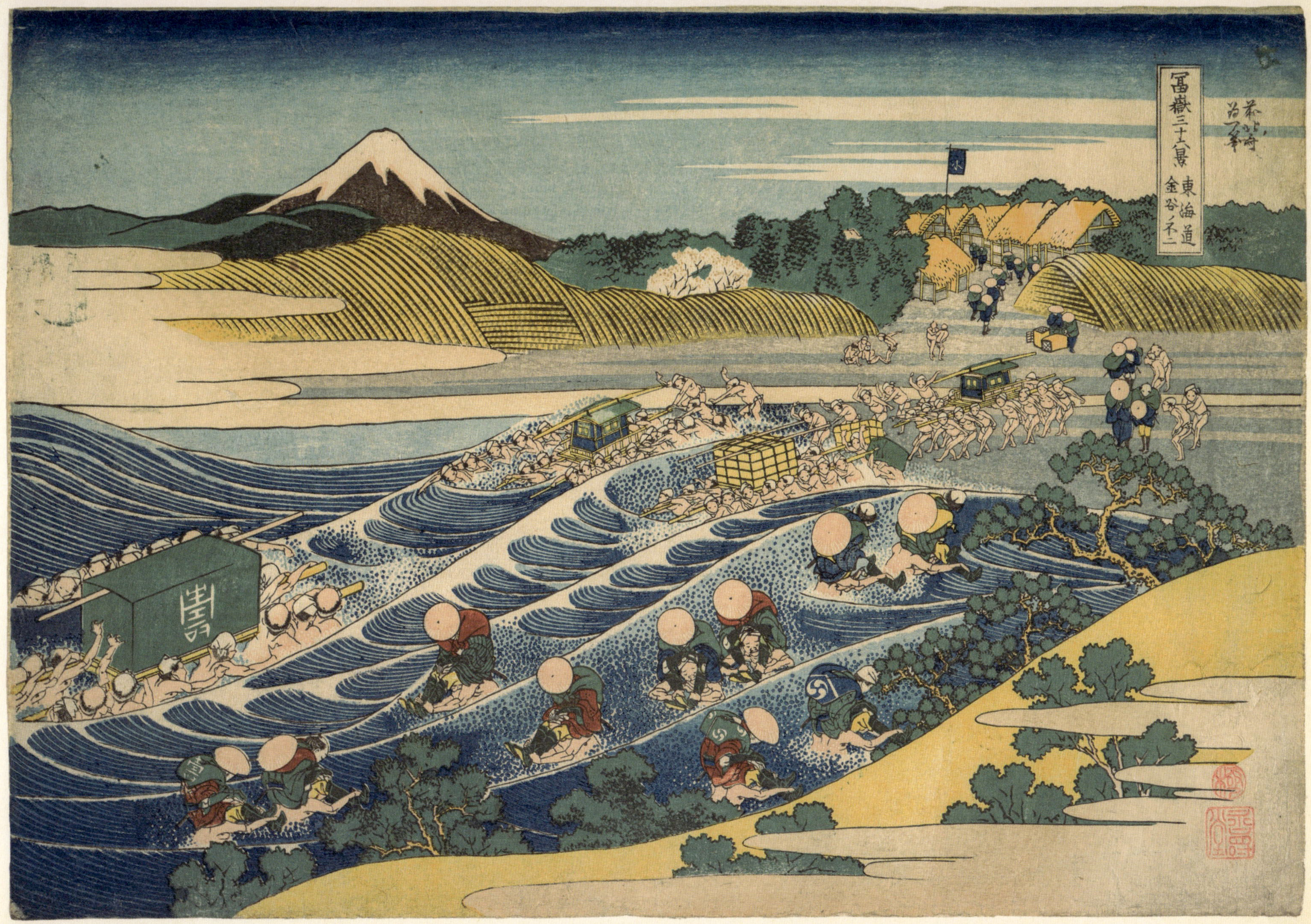

冨嶽三十六景　東海道金谷ノ不二
前北斎為一筆

Groups of Mountain Climbers

Shojin Tozan

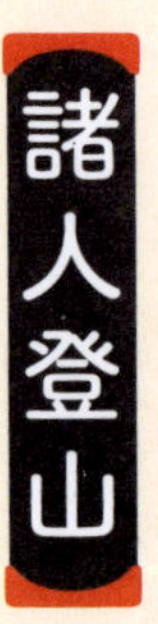

This monumental series ends with the only print that does not feature Fuji's unmistakable silhouette. Instead, Hokusai takes us up close onto the mountain itself, alongside a group of pilgrims who, with the help of walking sticks and ladders, struggle up the rugged volcanic rock, climbing and resting intermittently. Tucked away at the top right is a cave—which looks like an art frame—where pilgrims who arrived earlier huddle together in the morning cold. The color palette is dominated by the red hues of impending dawn and the deep brown of the volcanic stone.

Fuji was admired for its height, beauty and inaccessibility. Every year, groups dedicated to worshiping it would climb the mountain, dressed in white and equipped with staffs.

In his later series, *One Hundred Views of Mount Fuji* (*Fugaku hyakkei*), Hokusai also depicts the volcano from the perspective of climbers. Print #76—*Circling the Crater of Fuji* (*Hakkai-meguri no Fuji*), see page 123, follows a line of pilgrims circling around the crater facing the harsh conditions of the mountain with tenacity and determination.

In the current print, the travelers are depicted on three different levels, conveying a sense of depth, distance and movement. Their positions are reminiscent of another famous work by Hokusai, his *Manga* sketchbooks, which displays his incredible talent for depicting human forms across a multifaceted array of postures and activities (see page 122 top left).

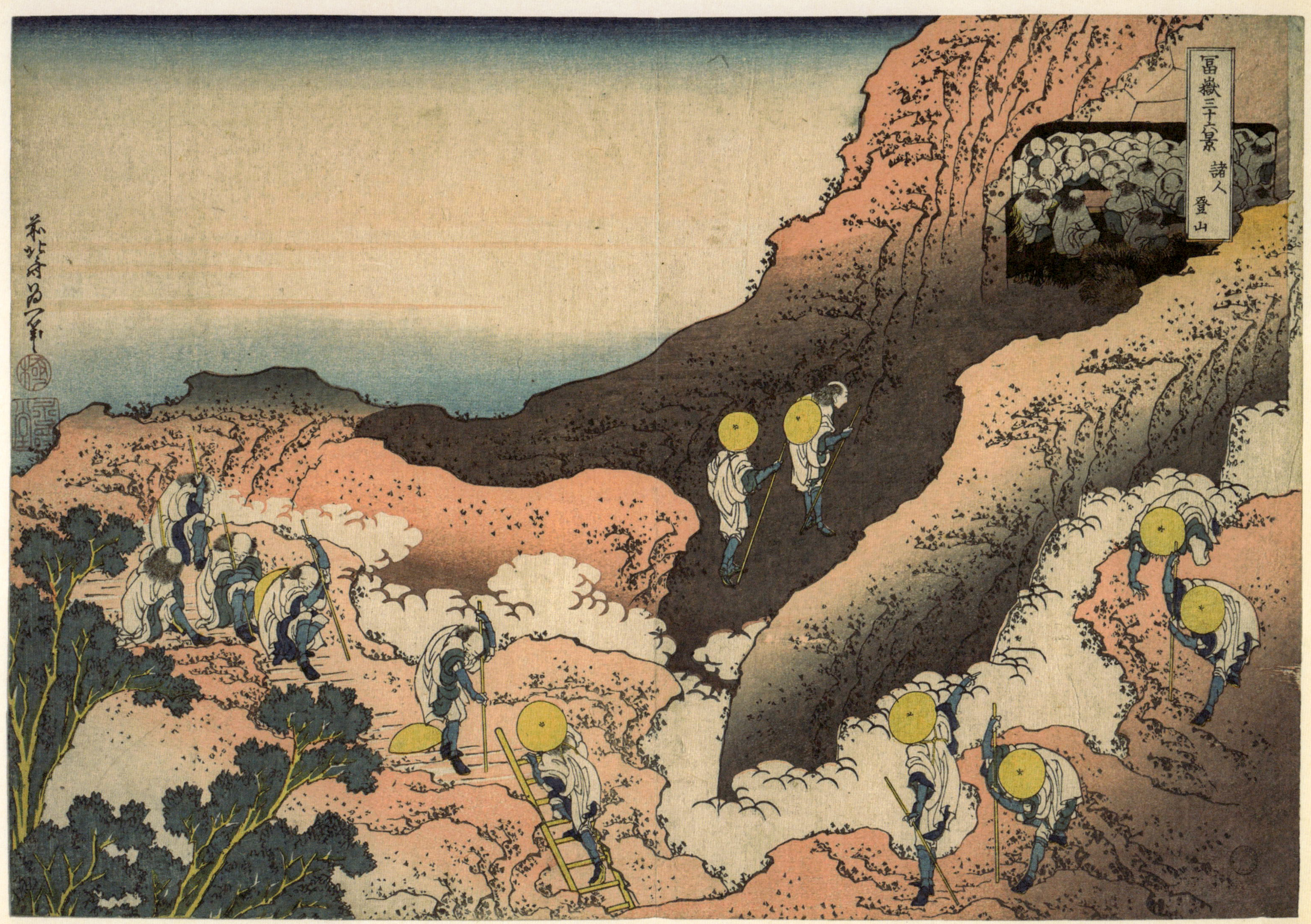

冨嶽三十六景　諸人登山

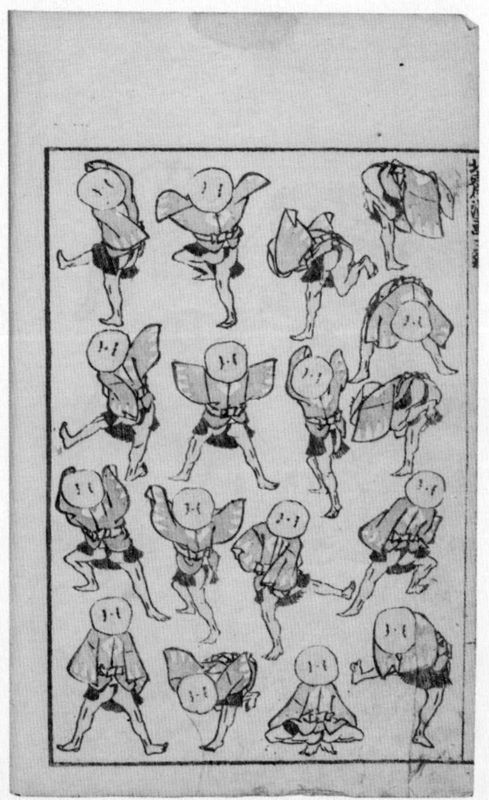 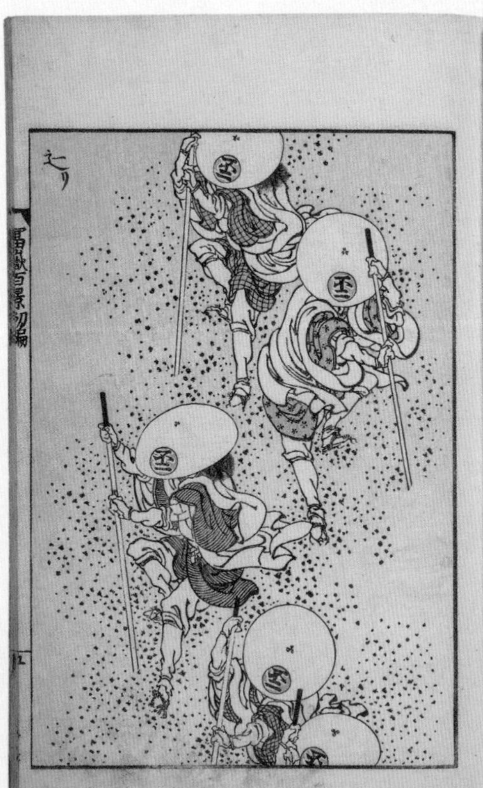 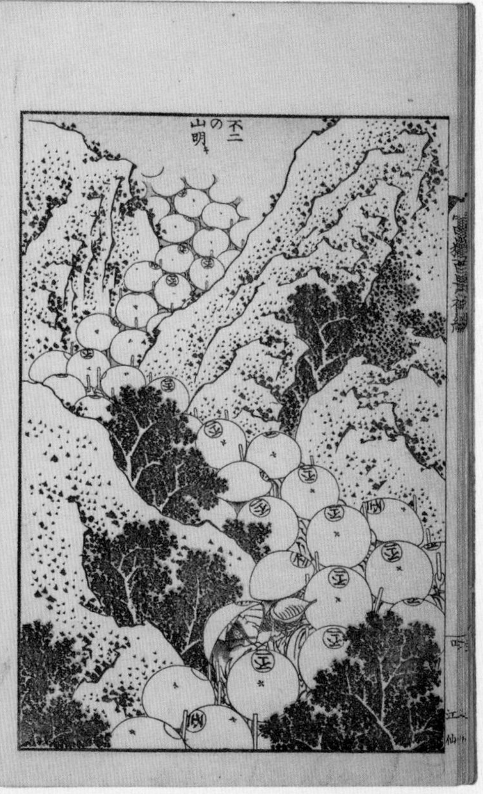

Prints #5 and #6 in *One Hundred Views of Mount Fuji*—respectively titled *Opening of Fuji* (*Fuji no yamaaki*) and *Sliding Down* (*Suberi*)— adopt a different viewpoint of the climb to the summit. In #5 (top right image), pilgrims in round hats undertake the first ritual ascent of the year on the first day of the sixth month. The circular shapes embedded in the volcano's rocky crevices lends an abstract feel to the print. A lone pilgrim at the bottom reveals his face, representing the human element that would otherwise remain in our imagination. He plays the *horogai*, a large shell used as a musical and religious instrument.

In stark juxtaposition, Print #6 (top middle) is a close-up of five climbers coming down the mountain. Descending the perilous volcanic scree, they lean on sticks to avoid slipping down the steep slope. The two images engage in a contrasting dialogue between ascent and descent, calm and chaos. "Fuji" is written on all the hats as: 不二 (peerless/without equal).

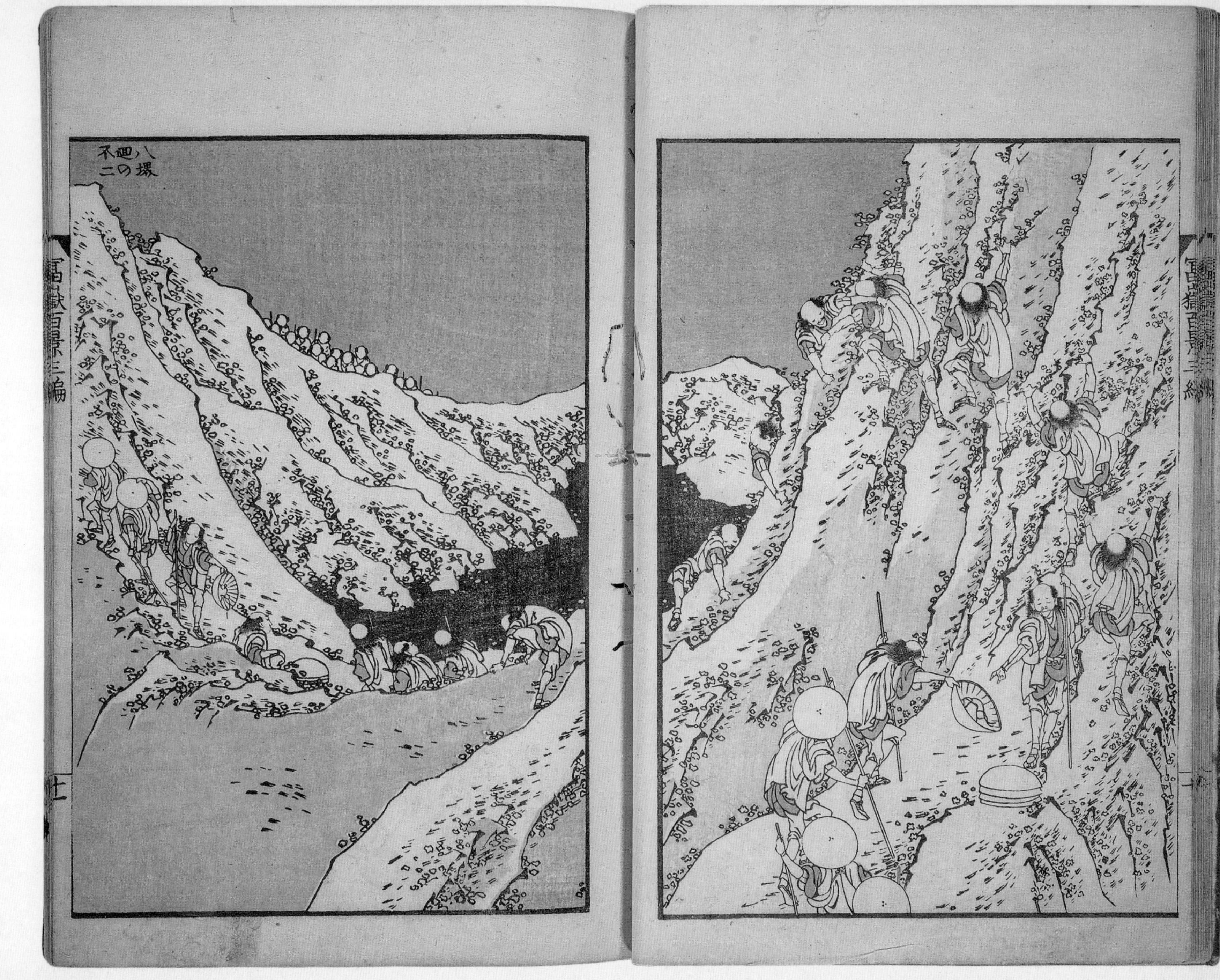

八ツ塚の
不廻二
冨嶽百景三編

Glossary

Aizuri-e 藍摺り絵 "Blue printed pictures." Works printed entirely or predominantly in blue (*beroai*), with potential additions of red and yellow. Effects of light and shadow are achieved through color gradation or with shading through the *bokashi* technique.

Beroai ベロ藍 "Berlin blue." The term for Prussian blue, the first synthetic pigment in history, created in Germany in 1704 and imported to Japan in 1829. *Beroai* was immediately preferred over natural dyes because of its intense color and greater durability.

Bokashi ぼかし An engraving technique that used shading to render the depth of rivers and the vastness of the sky. Instead of being applied evenly, the color was blended onto the wet wooden mold. The process had to be repeated for each print. Hokusai and Hiroshige popularized the technique.

Daimyo 大名 "Great Name, Lord." A feudal lord in 12th to 19th century Japan.

Edo 江戸 "Bay-entrance." The name for present-day Tokyo used from about the 11th century until 1868.

Fujiko 富士講 A form of worship dedicated to the holy mountain that arose in the early Edo period. Founded by the Shinto priest Hasegawa Kakugyo (16th–17th century), it transformed the ascent of Mt. Fuji into a religious ritual that symbolized rebirth, purification and the attainment of happiness. Because of the difficulty involved, only groups of brave young people made the journey up the volcano. Children and the elderly found it too arduous and women were legally forbidden from climbing the sacred peak.

Fujizuka 富士塚 "Mounds made in the image of Mount Fuji." In 1780, Takada Toshiro, the head of a branch of the *Fujiko* cult in Edo, had the idea of building a miniature replica of the sacred mountain on the grounds of a local Shintoist shrine. Followers who could not ascend the real mountain— due to age, sickness or gender— were thus given the opportunity to climb this miniature, scale-down version. The first *Fujizuka* was 33 feet (10 meters) high. Tanaka and his followers are said to have taken more than nine years to complete it because they used rust-colored volcanic rock brought to the capital from the real Fuji. Known affectionately as "Takada Fuji," this first mound can still be seen today on the grounds of the Mizuinari Shrine in the Shinjuku district. The Fujizuka that followed were mostly concentrated in the city of Edo and were often lower than 33 feet (10 meters) and made of local stone.

Fundoshi 褌 A traditional Japanese undergarment worn by men and women. Made from a strip of fabric $13^{25}/_{32}$ inches (35 centimeters) wide and $94^{31}/_{64}$ in (240 centimeters) long; it was wrapped around the hips and coiled in the back, creating the effect of a thong.

Furoshiki 風呂敷 A square piece of fabric used to wrap and transport small items or gifts. It was often adorned with a family crest or store logo, thus also serving as a form of commercial advertising.

Gokaido 五街道 The five main roads that ran through Japan during the Edo period (Tokaido, Nakasendo, Koshu Kaido, Oshu Kaido and Nikko Kaido).

Hanabi 花火 "Fire flowers" or fireworks. The tradition of firework displays in Japan dates to the mid-18th century. Large events took place between July and August and were attended by huge crowds.

Hanami 花見 "Flower viewing, looking at the flowers." One of the most heartfelt traditions in Japan where people gathered to admire the cherry blossoms, a symbol of transience, vulnerability, beauty and rebirth.

Hanamichi 花道 "Flower path." A raised platform made of five-foot (152 cm) wide wooden planks that, in kabuki theater, passed through the audience. Stretching the entire length of the hall, it connected to the main stage on its left side. The *hanamichi* was used for acting, but it was also where admirers traditionally left gifts for actors. These gifts, metaphorically and poetically called *hana* (花 "flower"), give the platform its name.

Haori 羽織 A traditional Japanese jacket that stretched to the hips or thigh, typically worn over a kimono.

Hatsuyume 初夢 "First dream." The first dream of the year is said to herald good fortune in the coming year. The three luckiest subjects according to tradition are Mount Fuji, a hawk and an eggplant, in that order. Fuji was considered lucky for its magnificence, the hawk for its strength and intelligence. The word for "eggplant" *nasu* (なす) symbolizes great accomplishment because, written with another character (成す), *nasu* also means "achieve" or "accomplish."

Hayauma 早馬 "Fast horse." Messengers on horseback.

Hikyaku 飛脚 "Flying feet." Foot couriers who carried letters, documents and small packages along the postal roads of feudal Japan.

Horogai 法螺貝 A horn-like instrument made of large shells, usually from *Charonia tritonis* ("triton's trumpet, a type of sea snail), that was used for various, mostly religious purposes throughout Japanese history. Some modern schools in Japan still teach students how to play this ancient instrument.

Kaimami 垣間見 "Peeking." The act of spying—primarily on women with whom one often fell in love—through the cracks in the sliding panels of traditional Japanese dwellings. The practice was widespread among nobles from the Heian period (794–1185) onward.

Kasuri 絣 A Japanese dyeing technique where fabric was made from specially dyed fibers to create patterns that resembled a fuzzy or brushed appearance.

Katsushika Hokusai 葛飾 北斎 (1760–1849) was probably the best-known Japanese artist in the world. A student of Shunsho, a skilled painter and author of *ukiyo-e*, he portrayed diverse subjects, which included "views of famous places" (*meisho-e*) such as his *Thirty-six Views of Mount Fuji (Fugaku sanjurokkei)*. One of his pseudonyms was Gakyojin, the "old man mad about painting."

Kawamura Minsetsu 河村 岷雪 (17th–18th century) was a calligrapher and painter of the Edo period, and author of the four-volume *One Hundred Fuji (Hyaku Fuji)*, published in 1767.

Nishiki-e 錦絵 "Brocade Prints." A multicolored printing technique.

Nishimuraya Yohachi 西村屋 与八 (18th–19th century) was one of the leading publishers of prints and books during the Edo period. He founded the publishing house Nishimuraya Yohachi, known as Eijudo, the name also given to his shop. He published a large quantity of books and prints with some of the best artists of the time such as Hokusai, Eishi, Kuniyasu, Toyokuni I and Kunisada. He was a member of *Fujiko*, the cult dedicated to Mt. Fuji.

Oban 大判 A print size of approximately 10 in × 15 inches (25 × 38 centimeters).

Oshiokuri-bune 押送船 "Fast boats." Boats that were used to transport fish from the villages to Edo.

Sakoku 鎖国 "Locked country." The policy of isolation in Japan during the Edo period. It was not a complete lockdown, but travel in and out of the country was strictly regulated for both Japanese and foreigners.

Sankin kotai 参勤交代 "Alternate attendance." The system of political-administrative control in effect from 1635, under which each *daimyo* maintained a residence both in Edo and in his own fiefdom, and was forced to spend alternating years between each. When the feudal lord returned to his own lands with his retinue, however, his family remained in the capital. The *shogun* could thus control the feudal lords and the members of their families. The maintenance and travel expenses incurred from managing two residences weakened the *daimyo*'s economic resources, styming their capacity to revolt against the shogunate. On the other hand, the system also fostered strong economic growth in the city of Edo and an expansion of communication routes.

Sansuiga 山水画 "Mountains and water paintings." A traditional Chinese, Korean and Japanese painting style that depicted idealized or natural landscapes using brush and ink.

Shinto 神道 "The Way of the Gods." A religion originated in Japan that practiced polytheism and animism. It involved the worship of *kami* (神), deities, nature and spiritual entities such as ancestors.

Shogun 将軍 "Commander-in-Chief." The title bestowed on political and military leaders who ruled Japan between 1192 and 1868, reserved for the highest office in the country's armed forces. Although each *shogun* had to be appointed by the emperor, the inauguration was a purely formal act. His powers were equivalent to that of a head of government.

Shunga 春画 "Images of Spring." Erotic images painted or printed in the *ukiyo-e* style, with special reference to the works of the Edo period.

Suyari gasumi すやり霞 "Straight haze." A traditional (*Yamato-e* style) painting technique that abstracted clouds and mist. These graphic elements often served a narrative function, acting as a transition between two scenes.

Taikobashi 太鼓橋 "Drum bridge." A highly-arched bridge designed to be tall enough so that pedestrians could walk across canals while also allowing boats to pass underneath.

Tokaido 東海道 "Eastern sea route." The route that connected Edo to Kyoto by skirting around the coast of the Pacific Ocean. 53 post stations were established on this artery, high-lighting its administrative, economic and cultural importance. In 1619, the road was extended to Osaka and included four additional stations. This new segment was known by the names Osaka Kaido (大阪街道) or Kyokaido (京街道).

Torii 鳥居 The traditional gateways commonly found at the entrance to a Shinto shrine or sacred area, consisting of two vertical support columns and a horizontal mast on top. Usually painted in a reddish-orange color and made of stone or wood, today *torii* also come in steel or reinforced concrete. Their number can vary from one to many. Passing under them is considered an initial rite of purification.

Ukiyo-e 浮世絵 "Images from the floating world." A genre that encompasses paintings and woodblock prints in the Edo period whose favorite subjects were female beauties, theater actors, and famous places.

Utagawa Hiroshige 歌川 広重 (1787–1858) was one of the last great *ukiyo-e* artists. At the age of 14, he entered the workshop of the Utagawa school, from which he derived his name. He portrayed actors, warriors and courtesans, but above all excelled in depicting images of nature and landscapes. Along with Hokusai he was considered one of the greatest landscape painters of the period. His most famous series are *The Fifty-Three Stations of the Tokaido Road* (*Tokaido gojusan tsugi,* 1833–1834), *Eight Views of Omi (Omi hakkei,* 1834) and *One Hundred Famous Views of Edo (Meisho Edo hyakkei,* 1856–1858).

Yamato-e 大和絵 "Japanese painting." A decorative and traditional style of painting that developed in Japan between the 12th and 13th centuries, partly of native inspiration and partly derived from the ancient painting styles of the Tang Dynasty (618–907) in China. *Yamato-e* captured the beauty of nature through depictions of famous places or the four seasons.

Yukata 浴衣 "Bathing dress." A light and informal garment often made of cotton and worn mainly during the summer for events such as firework displays (*hanabi*) and onsen bathing in the *ryokan* (traditional inns).

Zori 草履 "Straw shoe." A footwear similar to flip-flops, often made from rice straw, cloth, lacquered wood, leather, rubber or other synthetic materials.

Bibliography

Balcou, Amélie, *Hokusai: Thirty-six Views of Mount Fuji*, Prestel, Munich-London-New York, 2019

Calza, Gian Carlo, *Le stampe del mondo fluttuante*, Scheiwiller, Milano, 1976

——, *Hokusai. Il vecchio pazzo per la pittura*, Electa, Milano, 1999

——, *Ukiyoe. Il mondo fluttuante*, Electa, Milano, 2004

Carpenter, John, *Hokusai and His Age*, Hotei, Amsterdam, 2005

Clark, Timothy, *Ukiyo-e Paintings in the British Museum*, British Museum Press, London, 1992

——, *Hokusai's Great Wave*, British Museum Press, London, 2011

——, *Hokusai: Beyond the Great Wave*, Thames & Hudson, London, 2017

Delay, Nelly, *Les cent vues du Mont Fuji*, Hazan, Paris, 2020

Forrer, Matthi, *Hokusai*, Prestel, Munich-New York, 2010

Harris, Frederick, *Ukiyo-e: The Art of the Japanese Print*, Tuttle, 2010

Kondo, Ichitaro, *The Thirty-six Views of Mount Fuji by Hokusai*, East-West Center Press, Honolulu, 1966

Lane, Richard, *Images from the Floating World: The Japanese Print*, Oxford University Press, 1978

Marks, Andreas, *Hokusai—Thirty-six Views of Mount Fuji*, Taschen, 2021

White, Julia M., Brandon, Reiko Michinaga and Woodson, Yoko, *Hokusai and Hiroshige: Great Japanese Prints from the James A. Michener Collection, Honolulu Academy of Arts*, University of Washington, 1998

Photo Credits

About the Author

Elisabetta Scantamburlo is a researcher in the field of Japanese arts. A translator and editor of volumes on the subject, after graduating in Japanese Language and Literature with a focus on the arts from Ca' Foscari University in Venice (Italy), she obtained a doctorate in Civilization of India and East Asia, investigating the influences of Zen on 20th-century Western arts, and she also conducted research at Keio University in Tokyo. She has been curator of numerous exhibitions of contemporary art and design, working with several galleries, and she has collaborated on some of the most important exhibitions on Japanese art held at Palazzo Reale in Milan: *Hokusai* (1999), *Ukiyo-e. Il mondo fluttuante* (2004) and *Giappone. L'arte del mutamento* (2005). She has written various articles on both Japanese and Western contemporary art and is co-author of the volume *L'arte del manifesto giapponese* (2021), with Gian Carlo Calza. For NuiNui, she published *Shunga – Immagini del desiderio nell'arte erotica del Giappone di ieri e di oggi* (2022). She also translates children's books.

Published by Tuttle Publishing, an imprint of Periplus Editions (HK) Ltd

www.tuttlepublishing.com

Original edition: HOKUSAI – Trentasei vedute del Fuji
Copyright © Nuinui SA 2024
Editorial Director: Federica Romagnoli
Graphic Design: Clara Zanotti

ISBN 978-4-8053-1938-3
Library of Congress Cataloging in Process
English edition © 2025 Periplus Editions (HK) Ltd

Printed in China   2501CM

28 27 26 25   10 9 8 7 6 5 4 3 2 1

Distributed by
North America, Latin America & Europe
Tuttle Publishing
364 Innovation Drive
North Clarendon, VT 05759-9436 U.S.A.
Tel: 1 (802) 773-8930
info@tuttlepublishing.com
www.tuttlepublishing.com

Japan
Tuttle Publishing
Yaekari Building 3rd Floor, 5-4-12 Osaki
Shinagawa-ku, Tokyo 141-0032
Tel: (81) 3 5437-0171
sales@tuttle.co.jp
www.tuttle.co.jp

Asia Pacific
Berkeley Books Pte. Ltd.
3 Kallang Sector, #04-01, Singapore 349278
Tel: (65) 67412178
inquiries@periplus.com.sg
www.tuttlepublishing.com